AMERICAN COMMUNITIES

This new edition of William Alfred Hind's famous
work on American utopian communities is an unabridged
and unaltered republication of the volume as printed in
1878. The complete original book follows the new introduction by Professor Parkes.

American Communities

by William Alfred Hinds

Introduction by Henry Bamford Parkes

THE CITADEL PRESS

SECAUCUS, NEW JERSEY

HENRY BAMFORD PARKES was born in Sheffield, England, in 1904. After attending Oxford (B.A.), he came to the United States and received his Ph.D. at the University of Michigan. Since 1930 he has been on the faculty of New York University where he is now Professor of History and chairman of the Department of American Civilization. His published books include *Jonathan Edwards* (1930), *Marxism: An Autopsy* (1939), *Recent America* (1942), *The American Experience* (1947), *The United States of America* (1953), *Gods and Men* (1959), and *A History of Mexico* (revised edition, 1960). He is Consulting Editor for the American Experience Series.

First Citadel paperbound printing, 1973
Copyright © 1961 Corinth Books Inc.
Citadel Press, Inc., Publishers
A subsidiary of Lyle Stuart, Inc.
120 Enterprise Avenue, Secaucus, New Jersey 07094
In Canada: George J. McLeod Limited
73 Bathurst Street, Toronto 2B, Ontario
Manufactured in the United States of America
ISBN 0-8065-0359-9

INTRODUCTION

The conception of the United States as a kind of messianic nation destined by God or by the processes of history to be the scene of a new and better social order which would be an example to the rest of the world, has always been a significant element in the national consciousness. The great seal of the United States, designed after the establishment of independence, bears the words *Novus Ordo Seclorum*, a new order of the ages. For most Americans this higher society is implicit in the American way of life. But ever since the first colonization the sense of a messianic mission has assumed more extreme forms, especially when it has been linked with the millenial beliefs of the more radical Protestant churches. According to Edward Johnson, one of the early settlers of Massachusetts, New England was expected to be "the place where the Lord will create a new Heaven and a new Earth." It was to be "a specimen of what shall be over all the earth in the glorious times which are expected." Jonathan Edwards a century later, encouraged by the wave of religious revivals known as the Great Awakening, suggested that Christ was about to be born again on American soil.

The hope of creating a specimen of the millenium, whether envisaged in religious or rationalistic terms, led in the late eighteenth and nineteenth centuries to the foundation of more than one hundred utopian communities. Their institutions varied from complete communism to private ownership with some social control, and from celibacy through monogamy to group marriage. Most of their leaders seem, by so-called normal standards, to have been more or less paranoid, and some may have been conscious charlatans. Most of the communities were short lived, collapsing after a few years because of faulty planning, incompetent leadership, and the ordinary human failings of their members; and they never attracted more than a tiny fraction of the total population. Only one of them, the Church of the Latter-day Saints, better known as Mormons, has remained a permanent part of the American scene, and this was able to survive only by repudiating the most distinctive of its original institutions. Yet in exploring new ways of living and new kinds of human relationship the communities made experiments which often had great sociological and psychological significance. And in the boldness with which they repudiated the life around them and tried to achieve higher forms of social organization they represented aspects of the American character which should always be cherished, especially at a time of strong pressures towards conformity.

It has often been remarked that the most successful of the communities were based on religious beliefs—only a strong religious faith could bring about the necessary discipline of individualistic impulses—and that they were

guided by leaders with charismatic and virtually dictatorial authority. This was conspicuously true of the Mormons. It was also true of the two communities which
deviated most sharply from normal life and which seem,
on the whole, to have been the most interesting: the
Shakers, and the Oneida Perfectionists. Both these communities began with the premise that the millenium was
beginning, so that it would be possible to find a new way
of life, free from conflicts; and both of them recognized
that the obstacles to harmony were sexual as well as
economic. The Shaker prophetess Anna Lee, a· shadowy
but appealing figure whose mystical beliefs seem to have
been sincerely held, was regarded by her followers as an
incarnation of God in female form, thus completing a
revelation that had begun with Jesus as the embodiment
of God's masculine aspects. Practising celibacy as well
as communism (an attitude probably derived from Ann
Lee's unhappy marital experiences), Shakerism endured
for a century and a quarter and seems to have given its
adherents an impressive serenity. John Humphrey Noyes,
on the other hand, who founded the Oneida colony in
1848, was rationalistic rather than mystical, except in his
initial belief in the imminence of the millenium, and
made no special prophetic claims. The most novel feature
of the Oneida colony was its attempt to end sexual
jealousy and possessiveness by a system of plural marriage, every man being the husband of every woman.
This by no means resulted in sexual freedom; mating was
directed by the community, and any special sexual prefer-
ence—falling in love, in other words—was regarded as a
threat to the harmony of the whole family. Despite the
control of individual feelings, the experiment worked
with remarkable success for thirty years, mainly owing

to Noyes's psychological insights and to his benevolent but dictatorial leadership, and was finally ended only by pressure from the government of New York State.

American Communities, originally published in 1878, remains one of the most valuable sources for the history of the whole movement, being based on personal visits to most of the comunities still surviving in the eighteenth-seventies and on conversations with their members. Its author became a member of the Oneida colony as a boy of sixteen in 1849, was for many years the editor of the Oneida weekly newspaper, *The Circular,* and continued as a director after the colony was transformed in 1879 into an ordinary joint-stock corporation. While he displayed a realistic awareness of all the obstacles to community living, he remained convinced that the main cause of failure was simply that it was too far ahead of its time. Communism, he declared, referring to the community living practiced in these utopias, was in accord with the teaching of the New Testament, and would eventually be recognized as the "ultimate basis of human society."

HENRY BAMFORD PARKES
New York University

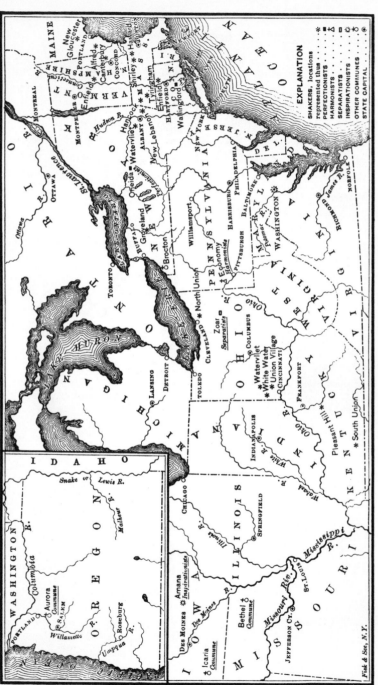

MAP SHOWING LOCATION OF COMMUNISTIC SOCIETIES.

Fisk & See, N.Y.

OLD CHURCH.

THE MILL.

BAUMELER'S RESIDENCE.

LOG HUTS.

STREET VIEW.

VIEWS IN ZOAR.

AMANA, A GENERAL VIEW.

THE BETHEL COMMUNE, MISSOURI.

TABLE MONITOR.

GATHER UP THE FRAGMENTS THAT REMAIN, THAT NOTHING BE LOST.—Christ.

Here then is the pattern
  Which Jesus has set;
And his good example
  We can not forget:
With thanks for his blessings
  His word we'll obey;
But on this occasion
  We've somewhat to say.

We wish to speak plainly
  And use no deceit;
We like to see fragments
  Left wholesome and neat:
To customs and fashions
  We make no pretense;
Yet think we can tell
  What belongs to good sense.

What we deem good order,
  We're willing to state—
Eat hearty and decent,
  And clear out our plate—
Be thankful to Heaven
  For what we receive,
And not make a mixture
  Or compound to leave.

We find of those bounties
  Which Heaven does give,
That some live to eat,
  And that some eat to live—
That some think of nothing
  But pleasing the taste,
And care very little
  How much they do waste.

Tho' Heaven has bless'd us
  With plenty of food:
Bread, butter, and honey,
  And all that is good;
We loathe to see mixtures
  Where gentle folks dine,
Which scarcely look fit
  For the poultry or swine.

We often find left,
  On the same china dish,
Meat, apple-sauce, pickle,
  Brown bread and minc'd fish;
Another's replenish'd
  With butter and cheese;
With pie, cake, and toast,
  Perhaps, added to these.

Now if any virtue
  In this can be shown,
By peasant, by lawyer,
  Or king on the throne,
We freely will forfeit
  Whatever we've said,
And call it a virtue
  To waste meat and bread.

Let none be offended
  At what we here say;
We candidly ask you,
  Is that the best way?
If not—lay such customs
  And fashions aside,
And take this Monitor
  Henceforth for your guide.

[VISITORS' EATING-ROOM, SHAKER VILLAGE.]

A STREET VIEW IN ECONOMY.

FATHER RAPP'S HOUSE—ECONOMY.

AMERICAN COMMUNITIES:

BRIEF SKETCHES

OF

ECONOMY, ZOAR, BETHEL, AURORA, AMANA, ICARIA,
THE SHAKERS, ONEIDA, WALLINGFORD, AND
THE BROTHERHOOD OF THE NEW LIFE.

BY

WILLIAM ALFRED HINDS.

OFFICE OF THE AMERICAN SOCIALIST.
ONEIDA, N. Y.
1878.

ONEIDA COMMUNITY — FRONT VIEW OF THE MAIN BUILDING.

CONTENTS.

SHAKER VILLAGE OF MOUNT LEBANON, N. Y.

AMERICAN COMMUNITIES.

INTRODUCTORY.

PROFESSOR HUXLEY, the famed scientist, in closing his address at the opening of the John Hopkins University, on the occasion of his visit to this country in 1876, uttered the following memorable words:

"The territory covered by these United States is as large as Europe, as diverse in climate as England and Spain, as France and Russia, and you have to see whether, with the diversity of interests, mercantile and other, which arises under these circumstances, national ties will be stronger than the tendency to separation; and as you grow more people and the pressure of population makes itself manifest, the specter of pauperism will stalk among you, *and you will be very unlike Europe if Communism and Socialism do not claim to be heard.* I cannot imagine that any one should envy you this great destiny—for a great destiny it is to solve these problems some way or other. Great will be your honor, great will be your position, if you solve them righteously and honestly; great your shame and your misery if you fail."

The condition of things here predicted as the result of increased population already exists. The specter of pauperism stalks in our midst. Hundreds of thousands of men are idle, while their starving families cry for bread. The problems which were to be solved at a distant day are demanding immediate attention. Communism and Socialism have already asserted their claims to be heard; not alone in destructive ways

—in revolts against established institutions, that are dreaded by the well-to-do classes as the revolts of the negroes were dreaded by the whites of the Southern States in old *antebellum* days; but also in examples of peaceful industry, general prosperity and happy brotherhood, which at least promise a "righteous and honest solution" of the great problem presented by our distinguished visitor. Moreover, these examples prove the practicability of forms of society whence shall be excluded pauperism, intemperance and crime, and all class distinctions not based on character itself. They are therefore worthy the careful study, not only of those who seek to bring the laborer and capitalist into harmonic relations, but of those who believe there are better corner-stones than selfishness and competism on which to build the society of the future.

If further apology be needed for offering to the public a new work on American Communities—a subject so fully treated by CHARLES NORDHOFF in his "Communistic Societies of the United States," and by JOHN H. NOYES in his "History of American Socialisms"—it may be found in the fact that thousands who might be glad to acquaint themselves with the results of practical Communism in this country cannot afford to purchase these large and comparatively expensive works, which are nevertheless indispensable to a thorough comprehension of American Socialism. It is not intended that the present work shall take their place; it is hoped, on the contrary, that it will stimulate the demand for them.

In describing American Communities the author has not deemed it necessary to commend any one of them as a model. The best of them but imperfectly illustrate the advantages of Communism, and some of them, it may as well be frankly confessed, have many objectionable features; but Communism, it should be considered, is only a child in years, while the forms of society with which it is brought in comparison are hoary with the frost of centuries. Americans say it is unfair to institute a comparison between their republicanism and the monarchism of Europe, and award the premium to the latter on the ground that it has produced the most perfect results in literature and the arts. "You must wait," they insist, "a century or two longer before you contrast the fruits of republicanism and monarchy. We are still engaged in pioneer work, and have given little attention to the higher departments of culture." So Communists may well say to those who would decry their system because it has not yet outrivaled in certain particulars systems that have existed for thousands of years: "Do not hurry the comparison. We have thus far been mainly occupied in rude pioneer labor—solving problems pertaining to our existence and subsistence—have been in circumstances resembling those of the early settlers of this country, who had to build their churches and school-houses while clearing the land and defending themselves from the attacks of their enemies. But give us a fraction of the time for development that other systems have had, and if ours does not then commend itself to all men by its fruits as superior to its competitors, let it pass away." Communism must take its chances under the universal law of "the survival of the fittest."

It is proper to add that the accounts of the several Communities which follow are, with the exception of Aurora and Fountain Grove, based upon the personal observations of the author, he having made a tour of the other Communities in the summer of 1876. He would nevertheless acknowledge his indebtedness to those who have traveled the same road before him, as also to many friends in the described Communities, who have rendered him invaluable assistance.

COMMUNITY DIRECTORY.

Amana	Community,	Homestead, Iowa Co., Iowa.
Aurora	"	Aurora, Marion Co., Oregon.
Bethel	"	Bethel, Shelby Co., Mo.
Fountain Grove	"	Santa Rosa, Sonoma Co., Cal.
Salem-on-Erie	"	Brocton, Chautauqua Co., N. Y.
Harmony	"	Economy, Beaver Co., Penn.
Icarian	"	Corning, Adams Co., Iowa.
Oneida	"	Oneida, Madison Co., N. Y.
Wallingford	"	Wallingford, New Haven Co., Conn.
Zoar	"	Zoar, Tuscarawas Co., Ohio.
Alfred*	"	Alfred, York Co., Me.
Canterbury	"	Shaker Village, Merrimack Co., N. H.
Enfield	"	Enfield, Grafton Co., N. H.
Enfield	"	Thompsonville, Hartford Co., Conn.
Gloucester	"	W. Gloucester, Cumberland Co., Me.
Groveland	"	Sonyea, Livingston Co., N. Y.
Hancock	"	West Pittsfield, Berkshire Co., Mass.
Harvard	"	Ayer, Middlesex Co., Mass.
Mt. Lebanon	"	Mt. Lebanon, Columbia Co., N. Y.
North Union	"	Cleveland, Cuyahoga Co., Ohio.
Pleasant Hill	"	Pleasant Hill, Mercer Co., Ky.
Shirley	"	Shirley Village, Middlesex Co., Mass.
South Union	"	South Union, Logan Co., Ky.
Union Village	"	Lebanon, Warren Co., Ohio.
Watervliet	"	Shakers, Albany Co., N. Y.
Watervliet	"	Preston, Hamilton Co., Ohio.
Whitewater	"	Dayton, Montgomery Co., Ohio.

-----

* Alfred and the Communities following are of Shaker origin.

THE HARMONISTS.

WHEN the Duke of Saxe-Weimar visited Economy, half a century ago, it was at its point of greatest prosperity. It had a thousand inhabitants. Every house was occupied, every factory fully manned. There was a fine museum, costly paintings (one of which, "Christ Healing the Sick," by Benjamin West, now ornaments the house built for George Rapp), and much attention was given to music. Sixty or seventy girls, the Duke says, collected in one of the factory rooms, and, with their venerated founder seated in their midst, sang their spiritual and other songs in a delightful manner. "With real emotion did I witness this interesting scene. Their factories and work-shops," he goes on to say, "were warmed during the winter by means of pipes connected with the steam-engine; and all the workmen had very healthy complexions, and moved me deeply by the warm-hearted friendliness with which they saluted the elder Rapp. I was also much gratified to see vessels containing fresh, sweet-scented flowers standing on all the machines. The neatness which universally reigned was in every respect worthy of praise."

Neatness still reigns in Economy, but in other respects there have been great changes. Many of the houses are now unoccupied; the factories are idle; neither cotton, woolen nor silk goods are made; the museum was sold long ago; their musical organizations are but reminders of those of yore; and the voices of the singing-girls no longer delight the visitor as they delighted the Duke of Saxe-Weimar. The thousand members are reduced to one hundred, and of these but few are under sixty ; and many have reached a great age. Their founder set them an example of extreme longevity (living in the full possession of his faculties till he was ninety) which his followers are emulating. Their present leader, Jacob Henrici, is seventy-three, and his associate, Jonathan Lenz, seventy.

The first impression made upon the visitor at Economy is that both architecture and people are un-American. It is the most natural thing in the world, as you walk its streets, to imagine yourself in some old town in Germany. But if every thing is foreign and unfamiliar, it is not unpleasing. It is seen at a glance that the village is laid out with regularity. The streets run parallel with the course of "the beautiful river" at this point or at right angles with it. Their houses are made pleasant to look at by the skillful training of grape-vines between the windows of their two stories. The streets, too, are well shaded, and shade-trees have also been carefully planted along the river's bank. Each house has its garden; and there is also a Community garden or pleasure-ground, in the rear of the old Rapp house. Here are beautiful flowers, winding paths, a fountain, arbors and fruit-trees ; and near the center the Grotto, which, like that at their previous home on the Wabash, is purposely made rough and unattractive in its exterior, while its interior is a beautiful miniature temple— thus symbolizing the fact that men's hearts should be better than their external appearance. A little out of the village still stands the Round House, which formed the center of the Labyrinth—so called because the house was so carefully concealed by hedges and vines, and there were so many paths crossing and recrossing one another, that the visitor might lose his way many times and waste hours even, before finding its entrance. Both the Labyrinth and Rapp's garden were great objects of pleasure and interest in the days of Economy's greatness.

The people themselves are now the most picturesque objects in Economy. Most of the men you meet are old and short and stout, wearing, for week-day dress, blue "round-abouts," like boys' spencers, and pants of the same color, and broad-brimmed hats; and as you meet them here and there they impress you as full of quiet dignity and genuine politeness. The women are dressed quite as oddly as the men, with their short loose gowns, kerchiefs across the shoulders, and caps that run up to the top of a high back-comb. The present dress of the Harmonists I suppose to be such as was worn by Rapp and his associates when they came to this country, and continued from choice by them and their successors.

But however much you may be surprised at their strange and unfashionable attire, the briefest acquaintance with this people makes you conscious of their sterling virtues. Economy, industry, business integrity, hospitality, benevolence: these are not the things for which they should be most valued. They have a repose of character, a resignation to God's providences, and an unwavering faith in his overruling care, in comparison with which their untold millions are as dross. I can never forget the impression made upon me by their principal leader, Jacob Henrici, as he told me the story of his connection with the Society—how he first heard of it in Germany when a young man with a good position and fine prospects—how he prayed to God to know whether he should come to America that he might connect himself with it—how he obtained what seemed to him a clear answer in the affirmative—how, after he had made his preparations for the journey, his friends persuaded him to reconsider his purpose—how he again betook himself to prayer and the counsel of the godly—how he was clearly convinced for the second time of his duty to set out—

how, after his arrival in America, he first established his aged
parents in a good home before visiting the Society which had
attracted him across the ocean—how deeply he was impressed
by its life and spirit when he made the first visit—how he
pledged himself to Father Rapp to join the Community, and
then returned and labored for years to place his parents above
the possibility of want, before executing his long-cherished
purpose. He concluded his story by saying he had never
since doubted that it is possible to get a definite answer to
prayer. Mr. Henrici was educated as a teacher—is a lover of
music, and shows in many ways the unmistakable evidences of
culture; he strikes you at once as a man of genuine nobility
of character.

The main facts in the history of the Harmonists may be
thus succinctly stated: they were Separatists from the established church in Germany; their migration to this country
took place in 1803 and 1804; they first settled in Butler
county, Pennsylvania; in 1814 they removed to Indiana and
built New Harmony, purchasing 30,000 acres of land; ten
years later, to avoid malaria and bad neighbors, they sold out
their property to Robert Owen, and returned to Pennsylvania,
establishing their final home, which they called Economy, on
the eastern bank of the Ohio, about twenty miles from Pittsburgh in a northerly direction; and they have steadily increased in wealth in spite of all their removals and numerical de-
cadence; and now own, besides their village and estate at
Economy, much property in other places, having a large interest in coal mines and oil wells and railroads and manufac-
tories, and controlling at Beaver Falls the largest cutlery establishment in the United States. Wherever they have settled
they have made the "wilderness blossom as the rose," surrounding themselves with orchards and vineyards and the
best cultivated fields.

They eat five times a day, having three regular meals and two lunches, and do not limit themselves much in respect to kinds of food. One of the best dinners I ever ate was at their hotel, which was formerly a popular resort for visitors. They are industrious, but no one works hard. The women from choice labor in the gardens. In early times they went with the men to the field. There are a great variety of shops, but many of them are manned by hirelings. They have a common laundry where steam and machinery save much labor, and they also have a common bakery, from which bread is distributed twice a week; milk is carried to every door, and meat is supplied to each household according to its numbers; the store supplies other articles; but their necessities are few, for wealth has not spoiled their simplicity. That they are, in short, a healthy, well-fed, well-clothed, happy people, is most apparent.

There are a few things in the history of the Harmonists which are deserving of special study.

First, *the superior ability of their leaders.* George Rapp, their founder, had great strength of character, and maintained his position until his decease at four-score and ten, preaching only two weeks before his death. He is represented as of commanding appearance, being six feet high, and well proportioned; very industrious, spending his leisure hours in study of the natural sciences; easy of approach, and even witty in conversation; eloquent in his sermons; deeply religious—"a man before whom no evil could stand;" and very simple in his habits. I take little stock in the stories of his tyranny, though it is quite probable that in the early days his enthusiasm may have carried him to the extreme of fanaticism.

Second, *the relation between George Rapp and his adopted son, Frederick Rapp.* In this duality the elder Rapp was the dynamic; the younger the more conspicuous and expressive. The one was predominantly religious; the other a great lover of art in all its forms. The one was founder of a new social order; the other gave to that new order its appropriate external expression. Frederick Rapp was, in short, not only the business manager of the new kingdom, but its architect and beautifier. He it was who laid out their villages in symmetrical order, and designed their houses, and gave to them whatever ornamental features they possess; he it was who most fostered their taste for music and art; he designed the summer-house, made of cut stone, which stands in the Rapp pleasure-garden; and he, I have no doubt, was the chief designer of the intricacies of the Labyrinth, both here and at New Harmony on the Wabash. Without George Rapp there would have been no Rappite Community, but without Frederick Rapp it would have lacked many of its most attractive features.

Third, *their removals.* There is nothing in their history which more forcibly illustrates their unity and thorough subordination than these. It is quite an event for a large family to move from one State to another; but here a hundred families sold their all in their first home, and moved off into the wilderness of Indiana, and in ten years built a village, containing over one hundred and fifty houses, covered the hills with vineyards, planted extensive orchards, brought under cultivation three thousand acres of land; and then, at the word of their commander, and at the risk of great pecuniary loss, sold every thing the second time and commenced a new home on the Ohio.

Fourth, *their adoption of celibacy.* In 1807 a powerful revival of earnestness pervaded the Community; and they were led to make a fuller consecration of themselves to the Lord's service than they had done before. The younger members took the lead in renouncing marriage, being told by their leader and by the apostle Paul that "He that is unmarried careth for the things that belong to the Lord, how he may please the Lord; but he that is married careth for the things of the world, how he may please his wife." Since that date celibacy has been the rule among the Harmonists; and such earnestness and unanimity were there on the subject that it was not found necessary to separate the sexes, nor separate the parents from their children; and to this day the men and women live together in the same house, relying upon their religious restraints alone to keep them from falling into "temptation and a snare."

Fifth, *their disuse of tobacco.* At the same time that they adopted celibacy they agreed to entirely dispense with the use of tobacco. The "vile weed" was thrown out of the Zoar and Oneida Communities by a similar agreement of the members. In overcoming such habits as the using of tobacco a Community unquestionably possesses great advantages. It is easier in such an organization than in common society to create an enthusiasm for some specific reform which shall become general and carry all before it.

Sixth, *their great secession.* This took place in 1832. The previous year Bernhard Müller, who called himself Count de Leon, had joined the Community with forty disciples, persuading the Harmonists that his views were substantially the same as theirs. But he soon showed himself a veritable parasite; disseminating his own opinions with such shrewdness that within a few months he had a third of the members on his side, and an actual division of the Community took place—two hundred and fifty withdrawing, and taking with them $105,000 of property. They settled at Phillipsburg, not far from Economy; but it was not long before they had wasted their means and broken up their organization. The account published by

Rev. Aaron Williams, D. D., of this secession, shows that Father Rapp exercised little caution in receiving the bogus Count and religious impostor. A single letter filled with flattering words of praise of Rapp and his Community, and exalting the claims of his own mission as the " Ambassador and Anointed of God, of the Stem of Judah, of the Root of David," so won the confidence of the founder of Harmony that Leon was received with royal honors upon his arrival. Tarrying at Pittsburgh he sent forward two of his disciples to herald his approach. A public reception was arranged for him. "The minds of the people having been prepared by Rapp's preaching for the advent of such a personage, it was a time of great expectation with the simple-minded Harmonists. As soon as the coach approached the town it was greeted with a salute of the finest music from the band stationed on the tower of the church. The Count was met at the hotel and escorted to the church, where the whole Community were assembled awaiting his arrival. He enters in state, attended by his Minister of Justice, in full military garb and sword at his side. He is shown into the pulpit by Mr. Rapp, and all eyes are fixed upon him and all ears are open. He expresses the belief that this 'meeting is the most important since the creation, and that henceforth all the troubles and sorrows of the Lord's people will cease.'" But Rapp was not long in discovering the true character of Leon. Conferences were held two or three evenings a week for a month or more between the leading men on both sides. Leon read from his "golden book," and explained his views; but the more he explained the more apparent it became that his principles and objects were antagonistic to those of Rapp and his earnest disciples. Leon would have been obliged to leave immediately with his followers but for the inclemency of the season. Permitted to remain through the winter, he employed the time so industriously in furthering his own interests that, ere spring time came, it was difficult to determine who adhered to Rapp and the old order of things, and who were in favor of Leon and his new measures. The heads were finally counted, and five hundred were found for Father Rapp, and two hundred and fifty for the new claimant. The "tail of the serpent drew the third part of the stars of heaven, and did cast them to the earth!" said Rapp when the result was reported to him.

Seventh, *the voluntary destruction of their property record.* Under their original constitution it was agreed that in case any member should withdraw from the Community there should be refunded to him whatever property he brought to the Community, and a careful record of the same was kept; but in 1818 Father Rapp, who was one of the principal contributors to the Community fund, proposed, "for the purpose of promoting greater harmony and equality between the original members and those who had come in recently," that this property record should be destroyed; and it was accordingly committed to the flames with the unanimous consent of the Community. Thus was the bridge burned behind them. And who does not see how wise a thing it was, for those who would abolish all fictitious distinctions between man and man, and remove all temptation to return to the old world of sin and selfishness? Eighteen years later, in 1836, a radical change was made in their constitution, so that thereafter the property brought in by new members became absolutely the property of the Community, and no seceder could claim any thing "as a matter of right." But though all claims on the part of seceders are cut off by the new constitution, the Society is not prevented from dealing generously with those who leave; and I understand it is customary to make donations to them varying in amount according to time and value of service. A young man who had recently seceded, whom I met at Zoar, told me he received a thousand dollars when he left Economy; but this was undoubtedly an exceptionally large donation.

In defending the rights of Communities as against seceders the Harmonists have done a great work for the general cause of Communism. As early as 1821 suit was brought against the Society by one Eugene Müller, who had been a member, to recover wages for labor and services rendered. The suit was rightfully decided against the complainant, on the ground that in signing the articles of association he had formally renounced all claim of wages. But the ill luck of Müller did not deter others from similar attempts to obtain money, of whom the most notable were Jacob Schriber and Joshua Nachtrieb.

Jacob Schriber was the fourth son of Peter Schriber, who with five sons and four daughters joined the Society in 1806, all of whom, with the exception of Jacob, remained in the Society during their lives; but after the death of their father (who had died intestate, having long before consecrated his property to the Society), Jacob, "as one of the surviving heirs, took out letters of administration, and made a demand upon the Society for an account of the property of his father in their hands. Suit was brought before Judge Bredin, of the Court of Common Pleas of Beaver county, who decided adversely to the claim. An appeal was taken to the Supreme Court of Pennsylvania, where the judgment of the lower court was affirmed, after an able opinion by Judge Gibson, which is recorded in Watts' Reports, vol. 5, pp. 360–4. The legal principles decided by this trial were, 1st, 'that an association by which each surrendered his property into one common stock, for the mutual benefit of all, during their joint lives, with the right of survivorship, reserving to each the privilege to secede at any time during his life, is not prohibited by law, and that right of secession is not transmissible to the personal representative of a party to such agreement, so as to enable him to recover the property of his intestate, so put into the common stock; 2d, that a member of a religious society cannot avoid a contract with it on the basis of its peculiar faith, by setting up the supposed extravagance of its doctrines as a proof that he was entrapped.' "

The Nachtrieb case was still more important in its results, it having been carried to the highest tribunal in the land. This case was brought before the "Circuit Court of the United States for the Western District of Pennsylvania, at the November term of 1849; and it was charged that the complainant, having been a member of the Society, was unjustly excluded and deprived of any participation in the property and benefits of the association; and he prayed for an account of the property and effects at the time of his exclusion, and that his share be awarded him by decree of the court." This case lasted seven years. The most eminent council were engaged on both sides, the Hon. Edwin M. Stanton, Abraham Lincoln's Secretary of War, acting for the complainant. In the first trial the claim of the complainant was sustained, and the "Trustees of the Harmony Society were ordered to render a full account of the net value of all the estate of the Society during the twenty-seven years of the complainant's membership, in order that the court might determine the amount due to him as his proper share of the whole. This led to a protracted and tedious investigation before Commissioner Henry Sproul, in which the pecuniary affairs of the Society, from the very beginning, were minutely and inquisitorially examined into, and all their books and accounts, their methods of transacting business, the value of their lands and all other possessions, were brought under review. The final result was the issuing of a decree in 1855 by Judge Grier, awarding to the complainant the sum of three thousand eight hundred and ninety dollars, as his rightful share in the estate of the Society. The operation, however, or this decree was suspended by an appeal which was taken by the Society to the Supreme Court of the United States. At the December term of 1856 the case was finally adjudicated by a reversal of the decree of the lower court, Justice Campbell pronouncing the judgment of this high tribunal in an ably written opinion." Nachtrieb had signed a paper declaring, " I have this day withdrawn myself from the Harmony Society, and ceased to be a member thereof," and acknowledged " the receipt of two hundred dollars as a donation according to contract," which was regarded by the Supreme Court as conclusive evidence against his alleged expulsion, and as a bar to all claims.

The Rev. Aaron Williams, after describing these vexatious lawsuits, in which " all the private and domestic concerns of the Society were pried into, all their branches of business and the profits of each, all their religious and social usages, everything, indeed, which was nobody's business but their own, was impertinently, needlessly and inquisitorially dragged into pub lic view," says: "The result of the whole, however, was to the benefit and credit of the Society. They became better known and understood ; the extravagant estimates of their supposed wealth no longer awakened jealousy ; and especially, the unimpeachable integrity with which their financial affairs had been managed by the leaders, even though never called to account by the Society, was a refreshing exhibition of honesty in the use of funds which is but too rarely found."

Another suit, brought by Elijah Lemmix in 1852, after a protracted trial of three years, had the same result.

The Harmonists are very religious, making the salvation of their souls the one supreme object of their lives. They are thorough believers in the Bible, and regard the Second Coming of Christ as near at hand. Rapp expected himself to live to witness that great event. It is not likely that they will change their attitude on this subject. "We believe that God has called us and given us the truth, and we will wait on him till the end," they will reply to every suggestion of radical change of theory or practice. They do not claim to be a distinct religious sect, and have no ecclesiastic organization separate from their Community. They acknowledge no written creed save the Bible. They believe firmly in the possibility of an entire regeneration of heart through the grace and mercy of Christ. They regard Community of goods as an essential part of Christianity. They believe Adam to have been created in the exact image of God, a dual being. They are millenarians, believing in the final restoration of this earth to its pristine and paradisaic condition, and that, according to Rev. 20: 4, 5, Christ and his saints are to live and reign on the earth a thousand years. Their views in many respects resemble those of Böhn, Bengel and Stilling.

A great Hall is pointed out not far from the church, wherein are held their three annual festivals—the Anniversary, the Harvest Home, and the Lord's Supper. On these occasions there are singing and speaking and feasting ; and before the last there must be thorough reconciliation between all the members. The Harmonists also observe with special interest Christmas, Easter and other days.

In receiving members they require, like the Shakers and Perfectionists, a thorough opening and confession of the past life of the applicants.

The young people, on reaching maturity are allowed their choice between becoming full members of the Society (provided of course they are of suitable character), or going outside, or remaining and working for wages ; and more prefer the latter alternative than the former, though required in such case to conform to the customs of the Society even in respect to celibacy; but the greater number take the second alternative, choosing a life of complete independence with all its drawbacks to the restraints of Communism.

In respect to the future of Economy, outsiders have much more concern than the Harmonists themselves, who quietly wait in trust for the coming of the Lord.

In the mean time they are showing their liberality in many ways. They who ask for bread are never turned away hungry from their doors, and they have freely contributed of their means toward benevolent and educational enterprises. Though half a century has passed since they removed from their home on the Wabash, they have recently expended several thousand dollars in New Harmony, partly at least for the benefit of its citizens. Purchasing the enormous cruciform structure, used as a hall and assembly-room in the old days when their Community flourished there, they demolished the principal part of it, and with the brick inclosed their old burial ground, twenty rods square, with a wall four and a-half feet high and one foot thick, adding a projecting coping and iron gates dependent on solid stone abutments seven feet in height. One wing of the cross was allowed to stand, and constitutes nearly half of the present Institute building (125 by 45 feet), containing a large public library, Masonic Hall, and five large, well-furnished school-rooms. The village made some contribution, but for the present really fine building, of which the citizens of New Harmony feel justly proud, they must mainly thank the Rappites. The latter intended it as a memorial building, and from its façade stand out the words: "In memory of the Harmony Society, founded by George Rapp, 1805." I was told that one condition of the donation insisted upon by the Rappites through their agent, Mr. Lenz, was that the old stone door which was designed and executed by Frederick Rapp, the adopted son of George Rapp, should take its place unaltered in the remodeled building. His Highness, Bernhard, Duke of Saxe-Weimar Eisenach, in his "Travels through North America," thus speaks of it: "Over one of the entrances of this problematical edifice stands the date of the year 1822, hewed in stone; under it is a gilt rose, and under this is placed the inscription, Micah 4 : 8." This inscription has reference to Luther's version, which reads, "Unto thee shall come the golden rose, the first dominion," etc., and is also commemorative of a vision or dream of Father Rapp.

It is remembered to the credit of the Harmonists that during the war of the rebellion they contributed liberally "for the equipment of volunteers, for special bounties, for the support of the families of absent soldiers, and for the Christian, Sanitary and Subsistence Commissions, for the fortification of Pittsburgh, for the relief of the freedmen, for the support of soldiers' widows, and the education of their orphan children."

In this connection I may appropriately introduce the following story to the credit of their founder. It is said that on one occasion, when their necessities were great and their means were small, Father Rapp went to Pittsburgh for supplies, and was refused credit at the houses which had before trusted him. His heart was weighed down with sorrow; he wandered off to the river's bank, and sat down to weep and pray. A merchant of the city found him there, thus engaged, and inquired into his necessities. Being informed, he offered Father Rapp two four-horse wagon-loads of provisions, telling him also to borrow no trouble about the payment. The thrifty Communists were blessed immediately with bountiful crops, and soon paid the debt. But the story does not end here. Years rolled by. The Harmonists prospered in all their enterprises; and when a great financial hurricane swept over the land they stood erect while many houses toppled over. In the midst of the storm they learned by some means that the merchant who had so generously befriended them in their day of trouble was now himself unable to meet his obligations and threatened with financial ruin. Father Rapp welcomed the opportunity it offered. Filling his saddle-bags with solid coin, he rode to Pittsburgh, found his old benefactor, poured out his money before him, and told him he could have as much more if it were needed; and so the merchant was saved!

The Harmonists have achieved an important success. They have maintained their principles in their integrity for three-quarters of a century, and have steadily increased their property until they are now millionaires of an unknown degree. They have failed in other important respects; they have not kept their numbers good in their single Community, and have attempted no system of propagandism. It remains for the Communists of the future to emulate all that is worthy in their experiment, correct their mistakes, and multiply communal villages which shall be as happy and prosperous as Economy was in its halcyon days.

THE Zoar Communists, like the Harmonists, whom they in many respects resemble, came to this country from old Würtemberg, which, during the early part of the century, appears to have been a veritable hot bed of religious radicalisms.

Both the followers of George Rapp and of Joseph Baume ler were called Separatists, but the latter were Separatists in a double sense, renouncing allegiance to both church and state, considering that they together constituted the great Babylon, which was to be "thrown down," as mentioned in the Revelation. They were, of course, persecuted and driven from place to place. One of their leaders, Johannes Goesele, was imprisoned for nine years; but his spirit remained unbroken. It is related that when, upon one occasion, he was brought before the Emperor Napoleon by the Duke of Wür temburg, at the former's request, he boldly warned the great soldier of "the dread account he would have to render in the great day for the multitude of souls he was hurrying into eternity by his bloody wars. Napoleon was offended, and de sired that Goesele should be punished for his insolence; but as soon as he had departed the Duke summoned his prisoner before him, and instead of punishing him said: 'Goesele, if you had not talked to the Emperor just as you talked to me I would have taken off your head; but now, since you treat us both alike, you may go home;' and he was accordingly set at liberty."

In 1803 George Rapp led his followers into the forests of

Pennsylvania, and founded, two years later, the Community at Harmony. The followers of Baumeler and Goesele endured the trials and horrors of persecution fourteen years longer ere they followed the example of their brother Separatists and founded a settlement in the neighboring wilds of Ohio, on the very ground visited by Rapp when seeking a location for his Community. But the Separatists who founded Zoar had at first no idea of establishing a Community. Like the English Separatists who settled at Plymouth, they left their native land that they might enjoy religious liberty for themselves and rear their children in right ways. They landed in Philadelphia in the month of August, 1817, and four months afterward Baumeler and a few others, sent out by the company to take possession of a tract they had purchased in the wilderness of Ohio, built the first log-cabin where now stands the village of Zoar. But though the rich had shared their means with the poor in paying the expenses of the ocean journey, it was expected that after they had reached their final home each family would shift for itself. This plan, it soon became evident to the leaders, would not work. Some were unable to pay for their share of the land; others unable, from age or sickness, even to support themselves; and the consequent failure of their enterprise would result, they foresaw, unless they adopted Communism of property. This step was accordingly taken in 1819; and from that time they have prospered, until, with their 7,200 acres of land paid for, and their saw-mill, two large flouring-mills, machine-shops and foundry, woolen-factory, store, tavern, Iowa farm, etc., they are accounted rich —worth in popular estimation a million dollars—worth, according to their own more careful valuation, $731,000.

Immense fields of corn, wheat, oats, and other crops are seen on their home-farm. They own a thousand sheep. Their herdsman took me over a two-hundred acre pasture to look at their eighty-five cows. I counted forty-seven calves in one lot; another contained thirty. A new cattle-barn was built two years ago, costing $7,000. It is 50 ft. by 210, and contains 104 stalls. The lower story is occupied for stabling and feeding. An asphaltum walk seven feet wide extends the entire length of the stables, and the fifteen feet separating the two rows of mangers is also covered with asphaltum. The cows, as they were driven up at night, made their way intelligently to their several stalls, where a "lunch" and the milkmaids awaited them.

Zoar, one has said, "is a little city hidden in an apple-orchard," and fruit-trees are certainly a conspicuous and pleasing feature of this Communistic settlement, as they are of nearly every other one I have visited; and so are the gardens. The German Communities are especially favored in this respect. Here at Zoar there is a large public or Community garden, much frequented, especially by visitors. At the center is a small circle surrounded by a thrifty, well kept cedar hedge; from which radiate twelve triangular beds, in which one may notice the familiar petunias, balsams, verbenas, amaranths, dahlias, geraniums, etc. Indeed, the several acres included in the garden are mainly occupied with flowers. There are, however, a few vines and fruit-trees, and on one side a green-house of moderate dimensions.

Aside from this common pleasure-ground, however, one finds few evidences of a love of the beautiful in Zoar. The buildings are mostly common in style and material, and include many of the log-huts and other structures of the early settlers. The house built for their leader, Joseph Baumeler, should, however, be noted as an exception. It is large, made of brick, has piazzas, balcony and cupola, and looks aristocratic among its plebeian neighbors; but it must not be assumed from this that the leaders of Zoar are themselves aristocratic, for Baumeler, I understand, was averse to living in the fine brick house, and Ackermann, the present leader, is unostentatious in all his habits, and occupies a modest dwelling. A common and attractive feature of many of the houses is a large piazza or double piazza, suggestive of hospitality and happy evening groups.

In criticising the appearance of Zoar, it should be taken into account that the people were, with few exceptions, from the common classes of Germany, and that they were at first very poor—scarcely able to erect even log-cabins—so poor in fact that they were compelled to put their means into a common fund, as we have described, to avoid the calamity of a general separation.

The people of Zoar are exceedingly frank in answering all questions relating to their Community life and history; and I can not perhaps do better than to introduce here a conversation between myself and a member who was for twenty-six years their school-teacher, and to whom I was referred for information by Mr. Ackermann:

"When did your Community reach its highest membership?"

"In 1832, when many persons came to us from Germany, including some who refused to emigrate in 1817."

"What was the number of members at that time?"

"I think it never quite reached five hundred."

"What is the present number?"

"Two hundred and fifty-four."

"How divided in respect to age, sex and membership?"

"There are fifty-five adult males, seventy-one adult females, and one hundred and twenty-eight children and youth under twenty-one. Of the one hundred and twenty-six adults, seventy-two belong to the second class, and fifty-four to the first class."

"How are these two classes distinguished from each other?"

"The first class includes the probationary members and the children, and all who have not signed the Covenant. After the children become of age they can not be received into the second class except on special application, and then only after a year's delay."

"What are the special privileges of the second or higher class?"

"The two classes fare alike in all respects, excepting that only the members of the second class can vote and hold office."

"How does it happen that so many adults still remain in the first class?"

"Some are perfectly satisfied with their present position and don't care to enter the higher class. This may in a few cases be owing to the fact, that so long as a person remains in the first class he can withdraw any money he put into the common fund on joining the Community, and use it as he likes; but on joining the second class there is an entire surrender of all property rights."

"In case a member of the second class secedes, is any part of the money he put in refunded?"

"No property is refunded; his bringing in much or little would not be regarded; but if he made application for something, it would be considered how he had conducted and how valuable his services had been, and a gift made accordingly."

"What is the position of women in your Community? Can they vote and hold office?"

"Our women, married and single, on joining the second class become full members, and have the right to vote as well as the male members. Our Constitution says nothing against their holding office, and in my opinion they could, should they be elected to an official position. They generally exercise their right to vote."

"What industries do they pursue other than household?"

"Besides milking, they spade, plant and work in the gardens, which you observe are connected with the houses, raising the vegetables required for family use and gratifying their taste for flowers. Those who do not work in the gardens, and are sufficiently healthy and strong, help a little in hay-making, and in harvest time rake up sheaves for the binders. In the fall they help prepare the flax which they spin in the winter-time. Some, who do not spin, knit stockings, socks, mittens and gloves, of which we sell large quantities in our store."

"How much hired help have you?"

"Including the families of those who work for us there are in all one hundred and seventy-one persons who subsist upon the wages paid by the Community."

"What is the effect upon the Community itself of employing so many hirelings?"

"Very injurious. They tempt our young people into bad habits. We commenced hiring about 1834, after the cholera had swept off about one-third of our old members."

"How many hours do the men work?"

"The able-bodied generally labor from sunrise to sunset."

"What regulations have you respecting the distribution of groceries, provisions, etc.?"

"Bread is distributed without limit. Meat (only beef), coffee, sugar, butter, etc., is distributed equally—i. e., to each family according to its number of persons; but we are not very strict in this. If a family is visited by outside friends it generally gets what it asks for. We have never eaten pork. Each family raises as much poultry as it chooses. If a family has more eggs than it wants it takes them to the storehouse, where they are distributed to those who have none or not enough."

"Did Ackermann, your present leader, directly succeed Baumeler, your first leader?"

"No. Baumeler died Aug. 27, 1853. As his successor we unanimously appointed Jacob Sylvan—a good writer, but no speaker. Christian Weebel read his discourses for him. After Sylvan's death, Oct. 13, 1862, Weebel took the spiritual lead; but the majority of the members were not fully satisfied, and in 1871 Ackermann was appointed, he being the oldest Trustee and having labored hard for the Society. We desired to honor him."

"What is the government of the Community?"

"There are three Trustees who regulate the work and all the business affairs of the Community—appointing such sub-ordinates as they deem best; but they are responsible to a Standing Committee of Five, whom they are to consult on all important matters, and to whom they make monthly reports. This Standing Committee is the central power of the Community. To it any one can appeal from the decisions of the Trustees."

"What is Ackermann's relation to the Trustees and Standing Committee?"

"Ackermann is one of the Trustees, but has no more power than the other two, and is responsible to the Standing Committee. He is regarded as a leader by the members in honor, as already mentioned."

"You referred to your Constitution: What are its principal provisions?"

"It provides that all officers shall be voted for by all the full members. It provides also that there shall be an annual election of one Trustee and one member of the Standing Committee; that a Cashier shall be chosen every four years;

and that the time of each election shall be published twenty days before it takes place."

"Do you still receive new members?"

"We have accepted new members up to the present time, and I think will keep on doing so; but our doors are only open to applicants of good character."

"What are your terms of admission?"

"We generally pay wages for a year or more to applicants, so that they may have time and opportunity to get acquainted with us and we with them. If the acquaintance proves mutually satisfactory, and they again apply for admission to the Community, they are admitted as probationary members and sign the Articles for the First Class. If during the next year they commend themselves they may make application for admission to the second class, and if there is no good ground of rejection will be admitted; when they give up their property forever. Rich people seldom apply for membership, and we are glad of it. We would rather take poor people, half naked though they may be, provided they have the right character."

"Your Community numbers only about half as many as it did forty-five years ago. You must have had numerous secessions. Have many of the older members left?"

"Only two parties of the older members that I recall. The first party left soon after the Society was established, and consisted of six men, all of whom save one were married, but their wives remained with us. In 1841 a grand scheme was planned for the division of the whole property. Many were at first in favor of it, and seven adhered to the plan, and sued for a division. They entirely failed in this. With a single exception they were worthless members. Most of them afterwards repented of their course. One was received back again, and allowed to work for wages. To two others the Community paid a pension of $8.00 a month in their old age and destitution. New members frequently leave, and many of the young folks leave as they become of age."

"I have understood that each family attends to all its affairs, its cooking, washing, etc., separately."

"That is the case now; but years ago it was not so. All the persons and families in one house did their work together. The present method leads to separation rather than Communism."

"Have you any very aged people?"

"Our oldest member is ninety-five years and four months old. He is a native of New Hampshire. He lived with the Shakers from 1830 to 1841, since then with us. Our oldest woman is now ninety-three. Both of these persons still work a little voluntarily, and both are unmarried. Another unmarried woman here is eighty-seven. A male member died last year aged ninety years and two months. Many of our members have reached from seventy-five to eighty years. Our factory foreman is past eighty-six."

"What peculiar ceremonies have you?"

"None at all."

"How do you regard the Bible?"

"We believe in both the Old and New Testament, and in Christ as the Savior of the world."

"What great objects have you as a Community?"

"Our object is to get into heaven, and help others to get there."

"Do you expect your system will sometime be generally accepted?"

"I formerly believed it would spread all over the world. I thought every body would come into Communistic relations. I believe so still, but I don't know how far our particular system will prevail. In heaven there is only Communism; and why should it not be our aim to prepare ourselves in this world for the society we are sure to enter there? If we can get rid of our willfulness and selfishness here, there is so much done for heaven."

"That is a good point certainly; but have n't you confidence in the perpetuity of your Community?"

"I will not undertake to decide the question of its perpetuity. If God wishes to have it continued he will see that it is done."

"Joseph Baumeler was a remarkable man, I judge."

"Yes; when he was our leader we knew every thing would come out right. He had the superintendence of our business, and he was at the same time our preacher, and cared for the spiritual interests of the Community. He was also our physician. He was, indeed, a remarkable man."

"What rules of discipline have you?"

"We appeal to the conscience. What else can we do? We can't punish anybody. Formerly, if a member disobeyed the regulations of the Society he was not allowed to attend the meetings, and that was punishment enough."

"I have read that for several years the members did not marry."

"That is true, but it never was intended that celibacy should be a permanent principle of the Community. The change from celibacy to marriage was made more than forty years ago, and a principal argument in favor of the change was that we might raise our own members. We supposed that children born in the Society would become natural Communists."

For fifteen years after the Zoarites began to marry it was a rule that their children should be taken care of by the Society from the time they were three years old, and they were for this purpose placed under superintendents appointed by the Community. "It was better so," said Ackermann, and

so said others. The abrogation of this rule was evidently a
backward step in the direction of familism.

A school is maintained at Zoar both summer and winter,
one of the teachers being hired from the outside world.
Music is cultivated. They have pianos in their houses, a
small organ in their church, and a band. They have also a
hymn-book of their own production.

I have spoken of the Zoarites as in some respects resembling the Harmonists; in other respects they resemble the
Quakers, by whom they were aided to emigrate to the United
States and to purchase on favorable terms their present domain. There is at Zoar the same aversion to ceremony that
one finds among the Quakers, the same freedom from secta-
rianism, the same simplicity of address toward friends and
strangers, calling each other by the first name if they choose
and saying "thou" to all, the same freedom to keep the head covered in the presence of dignitaries and in church, and the same
aversion to war; for "a true Christian," said Baumeler, "cannot murder his enemy, much less his friend." As among the
Quakers, only the mutual consent of the contracting parties is
considered necessary to the validity of marriage. They, however, usually consult the leaders of the Society, and formerly
the parties signed their names to a paper drawn up for the
purpose of satisfying the outside world. At the present time
the members are generally married at the office of the Justice
of the Peace. They hold that sexual intercourse, except for
purposes of procreation, is a great sin and contrary to the
Divine command.

These Communists are strong believers in the Bible as the
inspired word of God, and strong Trinitarians—believing in
God the Father, Jesus Christ the Son, and in the Holy Ghost.
Their explanation of the fall of Adam and of the original sin
is, that the primal man's imagination was thrown upon earthly

things; in other words, he wanted a wife, and hence lost the image of God. Therefore Christ had to come to restore again what Adam lost, and he is for this cause the Savior of the world.

The Separatists at first had a distinctive garb, but now dress pretty much as people do around them.

In the civil war they took no part as a Society except to pay their share of the taxes required to secure volunteers; and they would have been glad to have kept their young men at home at any cost; but fourteen of them were swept away with the current, to be killed, or die in hospitals, to absent themselves forever from the communal home, or to return begging for re-admission.

The Zoar Communists have had almost as much trouble with seceders as the Harmonists, and like them will be gratefully remembered in the far future for their efforts in settling by resort to the highest tribunals, regardless of expense, some important principles. Their Covenant reads:

" We, the subscribers, members of the Society of Separatists of the Second Class, declare hereby that we give all our property, of every kind, not only what we possess, but what we may hereafter come into possession of by inheritance, gift, or otherwise, real or personal, and all rights, titles, and expectations whatever, both for ourselves and our heirs, to the said Society forever, to be and remain, not only during our lives, but after our deaths, the exclusive property of the Society. Also we promise and bind ourselves to obey all the commands and orders of the Trustees and their subordinates, with the utmost zeal and diligence, without opposition or grumbling; and to devote all our strength, good-will, diligence and skill during our whole lives, to the common service of the Society and for the satisfaction of its Trustees. Also we consign in a similar manner our children, so long as they are minors, to the charge of the Trustees, giving these the same rights and powers over them as though they had been formally indentured to them under the laws of the State."

This Covenant has been the basis of two important legal decisions which Communists should generally understand. One of them was rendered by the Supreme Court of the United States, and settled definitely and fully, *that a member on seceding from a Community bound together by such a Covenant cannot enforce a division and distribution of its property;* and also *that a member of a Community with such a Covenant has no interest in the common property which on his death descends to his heirs at law.* The other decision, made in a case that was not carried beyond the State courts, settled another point of vital interest to Communities. It was held that neither a member who subscribed to the above Covenant nor his heir at law is entitled, in requital for services rendered, to a divisible share in the property acquired by the Community while he was a member, because "as between the seceder and remaining members he had already received all that his contract entitled him to demand."

Baumeler is generally regarded as the first leader of the Zoar Separatists; but Barbara Grübermann, I was told, preceded him in the leadership. She was a native of Switzerland, and was driven into Germany by a terrible persecution. There, in the province of old Würtemberg, she was received by a few people as one divinely commissioned; but died before her disciples emigrated to America; and Joseph Baumeler was then chosen as their principal leader. Barbara, had she lived in our day, might have been called a "trance medium." She occasionally passed from the realms of consciousness, and upon her return reported what she had seen and heard. These utterances were not written down, as in the case of the "Inspired Instruments" of the Eben-Ezer Society or "True Inspiration Congregations." Some of her hymns are however preserved, and I heard them sung in the church at Zoar.

The present leader, Jacob Ackermann, would be taken by a stranger as one of the common members. There is nothing in his appearance betokening superiority or any special ability; and yet he is greatly respected by all, and exercises a controlling influence in the Society. Although seventy-four years of age he still has the chief superintendence of both the lower and higher interests of the Community, and does more labor with his hands besides than many a younger man. In conversation with him you are impressed with his simplicity and sincerity. You feel that here is a man who can be safely trusted. He wins your full confidence at once. This, I take it, is the secret of his power as a leader. Then, too, he impresses you as a sympathetic, kind-hearted man—one who would willingly share your burdens.

This man is so sincere that he frankly admits that he is a little discouraged about the future of Zoar—discouraged because the younger generation do not come under the same earnestness that controlled the original members. They fall into the fashions and ways of the world, and will not brook the restraints that religious Communism requires. The unfavorable condition of Zoar in this respect may well excite reflection. Evidently it is not enough that a Community had a religious afflatus and intelligent, earnest men at its beginning. It must find means to keep that afflatus alive and strong, and to replace its founders, as occasion requires, with men of equal intelligence and earnestness; and to this end *ordinances* become of great value. The Shakers have almost daily meetings, and an elaborate system of ordinances that tend, we must suppose, not only to the maintenance of good order, but of the spirit which animated the founders of Shakerism. The Perfectionists consider their daily evening meetings and mutual criticism essential to their unity and progress.

The ordinances of the Zoar Community are few and weak. They have nothing answering to mutual criticism, and no meetings except on Sunday, and these are not generally attended, and are not of a kind to elicit special interest or enthusiasm. I was present at one of them. Not more than one-third of the members were there. The women sat on one side, the men on the other, both facing the desk, from which Jacob Ackermann read one of the discourses of Baumeler. The reading was preceded and followed by the singing of a hymn, with the accompaniment of a small organ. No one except Ackermann said a word; and he confined himself entirely to reading. There is no meeting, I was informed, in which all take part—where all hearts flow together in unity and devotion. Is it any wonder that the young people stay away, and that they lose their attraction for Community life? A Community should be an enlarged home, differing from the small home only in its increased attractions and its greater facilities for improving character.

Zoar, it must be borne in mind, is not a complete Community. Like Bethel and Aurora, it is a combination of familism and Communism. The property is held in common; their agricultural and commercial businesses are carried on in common; they have a common church and schoolhouse, and some common customs and principles: but each family has its separate household arrangements, and in many respects the place resembles more an ordinary country village than a well-organized Community. Their hotel is thronged after work hours with hirelings and Communists; and as the former drink and smoke and use rough language, it would be strange indeed if some of the Communists did not fall into the like bad habits. Experience shows that a Community thrives best when some check is placed upon the intercourse of its members with ordinary society.

In reviewing my observations at Zoar I am forced to admit that I saw there few signs of superior culture, and that many a village of the same size in our Northern States surpasses it in enterprise and in facilities for educational development; but when I asked, "What advantages do you enjoy over common society by reason of your Communism?" I got an answer that made me think their life might be richer and nobler than appears from any consideration of externals: "The advantages are many and great. All distinctions of rich and poor are abolished. The members have no care except for their own spiritual cultu: e. Communism provides for the sick, the weak, the unfortunate, all alike, which makes their life comparatively easy and pleasant. In case of great loss by fire or flood or other cause, the burden which would be ruinous to one is easily borne by the many. Charity and genuine love one to another, which are the foundations of true Christianity, can be more readily cultivated and practiced in Communism than in common, isolated society. Finally, a Community is the best place in which to get rid of selfishness, willfulness, and bad habits and vices generally; for we are subject to the constant surveillance and reproof of others, which, rightly taken, will go far toward preparing us for the large Community above."

BETHEL COMMUNITY.

I MUST describe things as they appeared to me, and say that Bethel has an unthrifty look. There is a main street, with a few side streets. Many of the old houses are of brick, plastered on the outside, and are badly scarred here and there where the mortar has fallen off in patches. There is scarcely a pretense for a sidewalk in the place, though the soil is of that adhesive clay which renders sidewalks so indispensable to comfort in walking. Grunting pigs forage every-where at will; and a big wood-pile, exposed to all the storms, encumbers the street opposite every house. Call the attention of the Communists to these things, and they will, with the utmost frankness, acknowledge that they are far behind the true standard and need many improvements; but they will add, that the present condition of things is mainly owing to the fact that for a number of years they have been watching for an opportunity to sell out their entire property here, that they may remove to Oregon, whither their leader, Dr. Keil, migrated twenty-two years ago to found the more prosperous Community of Aurora.

Still Bethel has many points of interest, some of which I will briefly mention:

First, Dr. Keil, so far away, commands apparently the full confidence of the members. "It makes no difference," one said to me, "in what way a man is troubled; if he takes the Doctor's advice he will find relief;" and I met no one who had aught to say of him in the way of censure.

Second, the young people are generally contented and stay

in the Community. "You could not whip them away," the elder members said to me.

Third, the leaders are men of great simplicity. You would not be surprised to find the President at work in the black-smith-shop or grist-mill; and the older members will tell you how Dr. Keil used to labor in the harvest-field, with coat and vest off, and sleeves rolled up. "Ah! he is a man," they exclaimed.

Fourth, the government is very simple. They have a President and several Trustees, who manage every thing, and strive to work in harmony with the general wishes of the Society.

Fifth, they have few distinctive principles; but those they do possess are certainly of the sterling sort. They make little account of formalities and ceremonies, and much account of a practical Christian life. They mean to live, they first of all say, as moral men ought to live, the elder members taking the lead of the younger in good example, as the founder of the Society has taken the lead of all. All strive to manifest their love one toward another; all willingly forgive injuries; all are esteemed according to their real character and not according to appearances; riches and poverty are abolished; the scriptural injunction which requires first of all obedience to God is respected by all. A man can be saved, they hold, only by becoming a "new creature" in Christ Jesus; and then if he has lied he will lie no more; if he has stolen he will steal no more, and if possible will make double restitution; and in all things he will seek to do good rather than evil. A man's whole duty, in short, is to do right and live unselfishly. To my questions about their constitution and by-laws, they replied, "The word of God is our constitution and by-laws."

Sixth, Communism and individualism are so blended that one is at a loss to determine which predominates. You pass along the streets, and notice the little houses and gardens, and you say, "This looks like individualism." You go into the shops and fields, and behold the men working together in groups, and learn that no accounts are kept of their labor; and you say, "This is Communism." You step into the store, and are told that the members pay for some things from the surplus of their gardens and poultry-yards; and you say again, "This looks like individualism." But crossing the street you enter the grist-mill, and see the members supplied without charge with whatever is needed for their households; and you say, "Here again is Communism."

Seventh, the line of demarkation between outsiders and members is not always distinct. Persons own property and carry on businesses at Bethel who have no interest in the Community. A small shop or store in the heart of the village is thus owned and managed by an outsider. The explanation of this singular state of things is found in the fact that about thirty years ago, only a few years after the founding of the Community, a partition of the property was made among the members, and a few availed themselves of the opportunity to withdraw their share from the common interest, and have since managed it wholly for themselves.

Eighth, many evidences greet you at Bethel of an earnest appreciation of communal life, in spite of its many unfavorable conditions. Here are a people who have fewer luxuries, fewer social and educational privileges, judging from external appearances, than the people of many common villages; and yet their testimony would be that of the old Brook-Farmers: "The life which we now lead, though to a superficial observer surrounded with so many imperfections and embarrassments, is far superior to what we were ever able to attain in common society. There is a freedom from the frivolities of fashion, from arbitrary restrictions, and from the frenzy of competition; we meet our fellow-men in more sincere, hearty and genial relations; kindred spirits are not separated by artificial, conventional barriers; the soul is warmed in the sunshine of a true social equality; there is a greater variety of employments, a more constant demand for the exertion of all the faculties, and a more exquisite pleasure in effort, from the consciousness that we are laboring, not for personal ends, but for a holy principle; and even the external sacrifices which the pioneers in every enterprise are obliged to make are not without a certain romantic charm, which effectually prevents us from envying the luxuries of Egypt, though we should be blessed with neither the manna nor the quails which once cheered a table in the desert. So that for ourselves we have great reason to be content. We are conscious of happiness which we never knew until we embarked in this career. A new strength is given to our arms, a new fire enkindles our souls."

Signs of comfort and substantial prosperity are by no means wanting at Bethel. Every house has its garden where the supply of vegetables for the family is raised, and where a few flowers gladden the eye. Every family has its pigs and poultry, and one or more cows. It was a pleasant sight to witness the incoming drove of eighty cows late in the afternoon, and see them separate to their several homes for milking. A large new brick grist-mill, standing at the lower end of the village, supplies the members with flour and meal; doing also much grinding for outsiders. The Community store furnishes them with clothing, sugar, coffee and other articles. From the tower of their substantial brick church a splendid domain is seen, of meadow, cultivated field and woodland. Some four thousand acres they have in a solid body, besides a thousand or more acres at Nineveh in an adjoining county, where half a dozen families live and pursue, in

addition to farming, some mechanical industries. Special care
has been taken to save their growing timber, or rather not to
wantonly destroy it, as is too often done in newly settled
countries. Their land is undoubtedly fertile, and well adapted
to grass, grain and timber. Their tables have an abundance of
well-cooked food. No fear of want goads them on, and they
take life easily. With their simple, economical habits they
have no difficulty in making a living even with their present reduced numbers.

Agriculture is their main business, but tailoring, shoemaking, blacksmithing, carpentry, coopering, and I know not how
many other trades, have their respective shops. Mechanics
and farmers command a premium at Bethel; learned men are
confessedly at a discount. The former they regard as "pillars
of strength;" of the latter "there is a superfluity," they say.
They do not seek highly educated men, because they have "no
need of them;" but they aim to give all their children a good
education in the common and necessary branches, and outsiders commend them as "well taught." They have no libraries, but valuable books may be found in every house, and they
subscribe readily to works that seem to them really useful.

They impressed me as benevolent and humane people, who
would not find it in their hearts to turn even a tramp from
their doors unfed. It is indeed a fundamental rule of their
lives that they "are bound to practice humanity, to assist one
another in time of need, and to worship God rather than
money." The President's home is also the home of the unmarried, the aged and the infirm.

Like most other American Communists, the Bethel people
are averse to war, and for this reason, during the great struggle between the North and South, many of their young men
emigrated to the Oregon settlement.

Bethel at one time numbered six hundred and fifty members; but so many have been drawn away to Oregon that it has now only one hundred and seventy-five.

The two Communities of Bethel and Aurora are considered as one, and are both under the presidency of Dr. Keil. His deputy at Bethel is Jacob Miller, who is highly esteemed by the members.

When a person secedes he can take with him what he put into the common treasury; and in case he contributed nothing on joining the Community, a small sum of money is given him on his withdrawal.

Monogamy obtains at Bethel; and the only restriction on marriage is that members cannot go outside of the Community for their mates, except at the risk of expulsion.

Religious services are held in the church only every other Sunday, and consist of congregational singing and prayer and preaching by Mr. Miller, the deputy President. The sexes enter at separate doors, and sit apart from each other. There is a high pulpit at one end, and at the other a space is railed off for the accommodation of the band on special occasions. The Bethel band, by the way, is described as such an excellent one that visitors come long distances to hear its music.

I cannot account for the fact that the Bethel Community has existed so long and with so much unity and prosperity, in spite of its loose organization and lack of clearly defined principles, except on the supposition that its founder possesses great personal magnetism and power over men. I know he is called by many a foolish fanatic, and is accused of things which if true would deprive him of all confidence; but it must be considered, on the other hand, that nearly every sect began its career with measures that were devised under the fervor of new truth and which the skeptical pronounced fanatical. But I imagine that in cases where there is actually fanaticism it is likely to soon disappear when confronted with the daily experiences of communal life; and certainly some remarks quoted by Nordhoff show that Dr. Keil has at the present time deep wisdom in the art of governing Communities. "In the early days," says the Doctor, "we used sometimes to have trouble. Thus a man would say, 'I brought money into the Society, and this other man brought none; why should he have as much as I?' But my reply was, 'Here is your money —take it; it is not necessary; but while you remain remember that you are no better than he.' Again, another might say, 'My labor brings one thousand dollars a year to the Society; *his* only two hundred and fifty;' but my answer was, 'Thank God that he made you so much abler, stronger, to help your brother; but take care lest your poorer brother do not some day have to help you when you are crippled, or ill, or disabled.'"

Fanatical or not, Dr. Keil, the Prussian man-milliner, after passing through the mysticism of Germany and the Methodism of America, when scarcely thirty years of age began his career as an independent religionist, and soon had a sufficient following to commence the Bethel Community. His disciples were all Germans and "Pennsylvania Dutch," and included some who seceded from the Rappite Community under the leadership of Count Leon, who, it will be remembered, founded a short-lived colony at Phillipsburg, Penn.

The results at Bethel show what Communism has accomplished among simple, uneducated people having the two essential conditions of religious unity and a leader whom all respect; but by no means what it can accomplish. It must produce the best results in all departments of growth and culture before it can make good its claim to stand at the head of civilization.

THIS Community, as already mentioned, had the same founder as the Bethel Community of Missouri. I did not visit Aurora; but I conversed at Bethel with those who had lived there, and have since received descriptions of the place from trustworthy correspondents in Oregon. The Community is located in Marion County, Oregon, about thirty miles from Portland. Although twelve years younger than Bethel, Aurora is the larger and more prosperous Community, having a membership of between three and four hundred persons, and a domain of nearly eighteen thousand acres. Dr. Keil, the President and founder, came here from Bethel in 1856, and it has since had the advantage of his personal superintendence.

The general characteristics of Aurora and Bethel are similar. They both resemble a common village in a newly settled country, only the houses are larger. At Aurora, as at Bethel, the streets, which are laid out with little taste, have an untidy look. The houses are constructed with an eye to comfort only, and scarcely any pains is taken to keep the walks and roads and fences in good order. Still there are signs of substantial comfort on every hand. The houses are surrounded with gardens, and each family has pigs and poultry in abundance. As at Bethel there is a common supply-store and a grist-mill which furnishes flour to all. The people have substantial food and clothing in abundance, but no ornamentation or luxury is seen.

Like most Germans the people of Aurora use tobacco

freely and drink beer, but drunkenness is exceedingly rare—
some say never occurs.

They work regularly, but never hard.

They have a store, hotel and drug-store, and all the shops
usually found in small villages, with a grist- and saw-mill, but
carry on no large manufacturing enterprise.

They have the finest orchards and vineyards in the State,
which yield good financial returns.

They have few accessions except from the parent Society
at Bethel; but their children generally remain in the Community on growing up.

They employ a few hirelings; and persons who propose to
join them are at first paid wages, and received on probation,
that there may be opportunity for mutual acquaintance.
There is no money condition in their terms of membership.

They attend church every alternate Sunday. Their religious service resembles the Lutheran.

Their principles are few. Their creed is as simple as that
of the apostles. Fear God, and do right in all things; that
is the formula into which they condense the whole duty of
life.

They have no written constitution and but few by-laws.

They are strict monogamists, each family having a separate
house, or separate accommodations in one of the larger
houses.

They have common schools, but give no attention to higher
culture.

The government is very simple. The President and his
few assistants, selected by himself, manage every thing.

They have few means of discipline, and little need of them.

They do not make great account of amusements; but they
have two excellent bands which go abroad as far as Portland
to play.

They keep out of debt.

The occupations of the members are generally determined by the leaders, respect being had to individual tastes and wishes.

The property is managed for the common interest, but each family has a deed of a part.

The two Communities of Aurora and Bethel are one in property and interest and principle; and for this reason a fuller description of Aurora is unnecessary.

Imperfect as the Aurora Community is, and uncultured as are its members, it can yet boast that "since the foundation of the colony it has not had a criminal among its members; it has sent no man to jail; it has not had a lawsuit, either among its members or with outside people; it has not an insane person, nor one blind or deaf and dumb, nor has there been any case of deformity."

AMANA COMMUNITY.

THE Amana Community of Inspirationists is the largest and in some respects most prosperous of existing Communities. Its sixteen hundred members live in seven villages near the center of Iowa: Amana; East, West, South and Middle Amana; Amana near the Hill, and Homestead. The last village is a station on the Chicago, Rock Island and Pacific Railroad, twenty miles west of Iowa City. These villages are at convenient distances from one another, and are surrounded by a domain of from 25,000 to 30,000 acres. The property of the Society is held in common, and is managed by thirteen Trustees, elected annually. The Trustees choose a Director, Vice-Director and Secretary, who constitute an Executive Committee of management. They appoint Superintendents of the different departments of industry. Besides their great farms, they have four saw-mills, two grist-mills, a tannery, a print-factory, and two woolen-mills. They have an excellent reputation both as farmers and manufacturers. They have hundreds of horses, more than a thousand cattle, and between two and three thousand sheep and swine. They make prints, yarns, flannels and other woolen goods that stand high in market. They are accounted very wealthy; but say themselves that their wealth is exaggerated, and that some years their expenses exceed their income. But "making the two ends meet" in such a great family, with about five hundred children under sixteen years of age and more than two hundred aged people, is a problem that may well tax their financial ability; and the fact that they are gradually accumulating property commends both their financial management and the principles that underlie their organization.

The members of the Amana Community are mostly from the middle classes; but they claim to have among them those who represent the higher classes of German society. One of the members contributed over $50,000 to the Society.

Several of the Communities—Amana among the number—have been transplanted once or more. The large Community of Oregon got its start in Missouri; the great Community of George Rapp—at one time a thousand strong—was transplanted from Pennsylvania to Indiana, and then back again after ten years, its roots being all the stouter for it; the Brotherhood of the New Life had its first Community experience in Amenia, Duchess Co., N. Y., whence it was removed to Salem-on-Erie; the Oneida Community was "potted," as gardeners would say, in Vermont, and showed few signs of large growth until it had been "set out" in the fertile valley where it now flourishes; and the Amana Community first took root in the State of New York near Buffalo, and there grew from 1842 to 1855. But land there was high, and they had at first only 6,000 acres, afterwards increased to 9,000! They wanted a larger farm, and so removed to Iowa and trebled their domain. It is an interesting fact to mention in this connection, that with their present enormous amount of land, located in one of the most desirable sections of this fertile State, they still rely for their income as much on their few manufactures, employing but a small part of their members, as they do on all the products of their broad acres!

The "True Inspiration Congregations" or "Inspirationists," out of which came first the Eben-Ezer Society and then Amana, originated in Germany more than a century and a-half ago. But there was no Communism until after their emigration to America in 1842. They say they were commanded by inspiration to live together and put their property into one common fund.

The Amana villages are laid out generally in squares, with a main street extending perhaps half a mile. The older houses and the greater number are of wood; those more recently erected are of brick and stone. They are of different sizes and mostly of uniform style.

The families live separately—one or more families in a house, according to size of families and of houses; but they eat in groups of from thirty to fifty. At the principal village there are fourteen eating-houses for the accommodation of its 450 inhabitants. Certain articles of food are regularly distributed to them. The milkman, I noticed, rung his bell at every eating-house night and morning. Food is carried in baskets to those who are unable to go to the eating-houses. They have three regular meals, and in summer two lunches besides, as at Economy. Their food is substantial, but unmodified by modern dietetic philosophy.

Every house in the village has a small plot of ground for garden purposes, in which you will generally observe, in addition to the common vegetables, a few flowers and many grapevines, from the fruit of which the people keep themselves supplied with home-made wine.

An allowance is yearly made to cover the personal expenses of each individual for clothing, etc. That of the men is usually forty dollars; that of the women twenty-five; that of the children from five to ten; but these amounts are increased in special cases.

There is a store in each village for the accommodation principally of its own people, but also patronized by the citizens of neighboring towns.

They have schools, in which the common branches and the English language are taught, as also their catechism designed for children.   The Bible, too, is read in their schools.

There is singing, but musical instruments are not permitted in the Society.   Neither are pictures nor games of chance.

They make long hours in summer-time, but "take things easy," seldom overworking.

They live to a great age, often reaching four-score years, and sometimes passing four-score-and-ten.

The women help in the harvest, doing of course the lighter work; and that women may have more time for public service there is a common nursery where two or three women take care of twenty-five small children, if there happen to be so many in a village, while the mothers of the little ones labor wherever their services are most needed.

Their working-force is directed by the superintendents as may be deemed best.   For example, during harvest-time the shop- and factory-hands labor in the fields.

They have some hundreds of hirelings, who are chiefly employed in agriculture.

The members all speak the German language, and a few the English.   Some came from Switzerland.

There are shoe-shops, blacksmith-shops, tin-shops, harness-shops, and all the common trades have their places of business.

They have three doctors, but no ministers or lawyers.   A dentist of Iowa City visits the Amana villages at stated periods.

They have breweries and make wine at home, and drink both beer and wine freely, but have no drunkards.

Tobacco is used to excess; there is smoking every-where.

The dress of the women is striking, but not picturesque. Most of those I met wore short gowns; and all, old and young, had on a black, close-fitting cap, tied under the chin and effectually hiding every ringlet; they also wore a kerchief spread over the shoulders and pinned across the breast.   The dress of the men has little to distingnish it from the ordinary styles.

Marriage is tolerated, but it is deemed best to remain single, as St. Paul advises. Formerly marriage was looked upon with a more unfriendly eye than at present; but a young man may not now marry until he is twenty-four, and he must still wait a year after he has announced his intention before he can lead his betrothed to the altar. By marriage the standing of the parties in the Society suffers for a time. If a man marries out of the Society he is excluded for awhile even though his wife might choose to become a member.

At table, at church, and at labor the sexes are separated.

This people are very religious. One of their rules of daily life is to "count every word, thought and work as done in the immediate presence of God, and give him at once an account of it, to see if all is done in his fear and love." There is some religious expression before and after every meal; there is a meeting for prayer every evening; there are meetings on Wednesday, Saturday and Sunday mornings. Sometimes they all meet together in the church; sometimes in smaller apartments and in order; for the members are divided into three classes: the first including the elders and the most earnest and spiritual; the second, those who have made considerable progress in conforming to the highest standard; and the third, the children, new members, backsliders and others. Their sole aim, they affirm, is to become true Christians, not only Christians in name, but true followers of our Lord Jesus Christ. They "believe that the same God who spoke through the prophets and apostles is still living, and in his Almightiness can reveal his will through the voice of a human being in our present times, as well as formerly;" and they are convinced that their inspiration "is the same word of God spoken by the Holy Ghost through the prophets and apostles, and cannot be influenced by the opinions and wishes of men." All their rules and modes of worship, they say, are given to them "through inspiration by our merciful God."

The "human being" through whom God speaks to this people, as they believe, is regarded as an "Inspired Instrument," and is the spiritual head of the Society. The "Instrument" is generally greatly agitated before coming under the heavenly afflatus, sometimes shaking for an hour. The Separatists at Zoar gave me a most sensational account of the contortions and tremblings of Christian Metz while on a visit to their Society, illustrating the manner of his inspiration. They were not at all favorably impressed by the scene. The line of inspiration has been continued, they claim, with occasional interruptions, from the beginning of the eighteenth century. From 1818 to 1867 there were two "Instruments" —Christian Metz, a carpenter by trade, and Barbara Heynemann, an ignorant servant girl; but since 1867 Barbara has stood alone in the prophetic office. She is now over eighty-one years of age. The people trouble themselves very little about her successor. "The Lord has always given us an inspired leader, and we can trust him for the future," they say in simple faith.

It is not easy to fully understand the entire function of the "Inspired Instrument." Its utterances are in general exhortations to holier life—to more thorough consecration to God —and in condemnation of sin and worldliness. Occasionally it calls the entire Society to some great step, like the advance into Communism after they came to this country, or to sell out in one place and remove to another. Sometimes it reproves individuals for their faults. Barbara is generally present at all important meetings of the Trustees.

Candidates for membership usually pass a probation of two years, but sometimes this term is shortened or even omitted by direction of the "Inspired Instrument." Most of the new members come from Germany, and occasionally the

Society pay the passage of poor families across the ocean who wish to join them. If a member withdraws from the Society, what he contributed is returned without interest.

Amana is a great example of Communism. Sixteen hundred people here live in comfort and happiness, each one sure of enough to eat and drink and wear so long as he lives—sure, too, of a home and friends—sure, also, of such discipline and instruction as shall keep him constantly reminded of the supreme importance of a temperate, virtuous, holy life. They live in such perpetual peace that no lawyer is found in their midst; in such habits of morality that no sheriff walks their streets; in such plenty that no beggars are seen save such as come from the outer world.

But with all its numbers and wealth, morality and religion, peace and plenty, Amana is still far from being a model Community. In many respects it fails to realize the blessings which belong to Communism.

Every one of its seven villages ought to have a few large houses in close juxtaposition, all heated by steam and furished with every labor-saving convenience, instead of its present scores of widely-scattered dwellings. A single kitchen and dining-room would then answer in place of the numerous eating-houses, and save much labor and expense.

Every village ought to have a butter-and-cheese factory; now each eating-house makes its own butter and cheese by hand.

Every village ought to have a common laundry, with its washing-machines and wringers and mangles run by power. Now each family has to do its own laundry work, and there is a public wash-house only for the unmarried adults. The building of a common laundry and furnishing it with the best machines is however in contemplation.

Every village ought to have a large library and reading-room. There is nothing of the kind. These Communists are not a reading people. They have some access to newspapers, periodicals and scientific works, but their chief attention is given to the Bible and their "inspired records;" and their theory is that education in other than such branches as are required in the common affairs of life is unnecessary. Their object is to save the soul; why, then, should they fill the mind with worldly wisdom?

But although the Amana Community have no considerable library of the world's books, they have a somewhat extensive literature of their own. They have a printing-press, and have used it in printing "Year-Books of the True Inspiration Congregations; Witnesses of the Spirit of God, which happened and were spoken in the meetings of the Society through the Instruments." They have printed more than a hundred books, mainly records of their inspirations, which are esteemed by them as containing words of Divine Wisdom. The utterances of their "Instruments" have been carefully recorded from the first.

With the exception of the flowers around the houses there is little indication that a taste for the beautiful in nature or art is cultivated at Amana. The monotony of the architecture, the entire absence of paint, the rough board fences which border the streets, the untidy sidewalks and other features, render the Amana villages unattractive to the visitor.

The interior of the houses is scarcely more pleasing. There is no ornamentation by paint or paper, carpets or pictures. Every thing is plain. Their churches and assembly-rooms have only long wooden benches for seats.

Amusements are not encouraged. There is no dancing or theatrical presentations in the halls of Amana. These they "deem a shame for all good Christians."

Their worship, too, has in it little that is enlivening—much however that savors of sincerity and earnest piety, and from which unquestionably the members derive inward comfort and strength. But the exercises contrast unfavorably with the spontaneity and freedom which characterize the meetings of some other Communistic societies. The men and women sit apart; and when a chapter is read, each one reading a verse, the women read after the men. There are no preachers, and little freedom in speaking. Sometimes the leaders discourse upon the necessity of holy living. Often passages from their "inspirational records" are read; and it is customary for all to take part in worship, by reading or repeating some short verse or prayer. When there are too many present to permit both the men and the women to take part, only one sex prays or reads, and the other waits till the next occasion.

The ascetic features of the Amana Community are in accordance with its fundamental idea and justified by it, namely, that people are placed in this world for the one purpose of saving their souls, and that this requires the crucifixion of such desires and appetites as divert the attention from God. This doctrine is at the foundation of all forms of ascetic Communism; and it is easy to see how those who accept it should look with suspicion on amusements, pictures, and social enjoyments. The people of Amana say: "He who made heaven, earth, men and all creatures could easily have been in possession of all the riches of this world, but he preferred to come among us as a poor child, and live as the poorest of men. He did not even have a place where he might lay his head. We, therefore, in trying to follow his example, have to lead a life of humbleness and self-denial, and seek to avoid all luxury, elegance, pride, etc., in our clothing, houses and surroundings. Our meeting-houses are plain, as our Lord does not live in houses of stone nor magnificent churches; he wants us to prepare and cleanse our hearts—'the temples not made with hands'—so that he may dwell in them."

The great body of the people are fully persuaded that their mode of life is pleasing to God.

Most of their youth remain in the Society.

They are non-resistants; they furnished no volunteers in the civil war, but hired substitutes to fill their quota. They, however, contributed during the war nearly twenty thousand dollars to benevolent objects. They take little part in politics, but in local affairs vote for the best men without inquiring to what party they belong.

Though the women work in the field their status in the Society is not, they claim, a low one. They have a council for the management of household matters; the recognized head of the Community is a woman; and all widows and unmarried women thirty years of age and over, who are not represented by male members, have a right to vote at the annual election of Trustees.

The Community do not court publicity, and complain that they are annoyed with inquiries and applications for admission. They prefer to go on their quiet way undisturbed. But the fact of their existence cannot be ignored, and ought not to be, in these days when the world is "in travail and pain" for better social conditions. If the sixteen hundred Communists of Amana have found a way to live comfortably, peaceably, happily together, while the world around them is in comparative misery, it ought to be known and read of all men.

There is one feature of life at Amana which might with advantage be adopted by every Community and every church. From time to time there is a general examination—"*unter-suchung*"—of the spiritual condition of all the inhabitants. Personal confessions of faults and sins are in order; and it is expected that the "Inspired Instrument" will throw light on hidden things. Evidently, such a cleansing process as this can have but the best effect on all who sincerely engage in it. How much evil-thinking, condemnation, and bad experience generally, such a periodical examination and purging might clear out of any social organization!

The Inspirationists, as well as the Harmonists, make great account of the Lord's Supper. The latter have constituted it one of their annual festivals. The former celebrate it only when directed by the "Inspired Instrument;" and then it becomes an extraordinary event. An account of the celebration of 1855 has been printed in a volume of 284 pages under the title: "The Supper of Love and Remembrance of the Suffering and Death of our Lord and Saviour Jesus Christ—How it was announced, ordered and held, by his Word and Witness, in four parts, in Middle and Lower Eben-Ezer, in the year 1855."

The Inspirationists have printed in one of their books the following twenty-one "Rules for Daily Life," which show how intensely (not to say ascetically) religious they are:

"1. To obey without reasoning God. and through God our superiors.

"2. To study quiet, or serenity, within and without.

"3. Within, to rule and master your thoughts.

"4. Without, to avoid all unnecessary words, and still to study silence and quiet.

"5. To abandon self, with all its desires, knowledge and power.

"6. Do not criticise others, either for good or evil, neither to judge nor to imitate them; therefore contain yourself, remain at home, in the house and in your heart.

"7. Do not disturb your serenity or peace of mind—hence neither desire nor grieve.

"8. Live in love and pity toward your neighbor, and indulge neither anger nor impatience in your spirit.

"9. Be honest, sincere, and avoid all deceit.

"10. Count every word, thought and work as done in the immediate presence of God, in sleeping and waking, eating, drinking, etc., and give him at once an account of it, to see if all is done in his fear and love.

"11. Be in all things sober, without levity or laughter; and without vain and idle words, works, or thoughts.

"12. Never think or speak of God without the deepest reverence, fear and love, and therefore deal reverently with all spiritual things.

"13. Bear all inner and outward suffering in silence, complaining only to God; and accept all from him in deepest reverence and obedience.

"14. Notice carefully all that God permits to happen to you in your inner and outward life, in order that you may not fail to comprehend his will and be led by it.

"15. Have nothing to do with unholy, and particularly with needless business affairs.

"16. Have no intercourse with worldly-minded men; never seek their society; speak little with them, and never without need; and then not without fear and trembling.

"17. Therefore, what you have to do with such men do in haste; do not waste time in public places and worldly society, that you be not tempted and led away.

"18. Fly from the society of women-kind as much as possible, as a very highly dangerous magnet and magical fire.

"19. Avoid obeisance and the fear of men; these are dangerous ways.

"20. Dinners, weddings, feasts, avoid entirely; at the best there is sin.

"21. Constantly practice abstinence and temperance, so that you may be as wakeful after eating as before."

One cannot withold his respect from these people for their religious earnestness, even though he may criticise their asceticism. Religion was their bond when they were scattered over the villages of Germany; it drew them together, and colonized them in America; it has held them together in the close relations of communal brotherhood for thirty-six years; it has given them peace and prosperity; and, above all, it has made their hearts rich in that faith which comprehends the mysteries of the inner world. Better reasons they could not desire for consecrating themselves wholly to the service of Religion. Some may think, as I do, that this is compatible with thorough educational drill, with giving much attention to music and high art, with freedom in amusement and all that makes life joyous. Others will think Religion itself can be dispensed with, and that all the Amana Communists have accomplished in their practical life, even their unity, can be effected through enlightened self-interest. But these Communists ask none of us to believe as they do, nor do they urge any to adopt their customs. And it remains for those who criticise them to show that equally precious fruits can be produced by other means than they employ.

It is often remarked that Communism may be applied on a limited scale with comparative safety, but that it will fail in a broader application. In the case of the Amana Society there is entire Communism of property, not only between the members of a single settlement, but between all the settlements. It makes no difference whether one village makes a profit or another, so that there is a gain in the whole Society; the people of all the villages are supplied exactly alike. If Communism can be applied with such beneficent results in the case of seven villages, why not over an entire county? Why not over a State? Why not over a nation?

ICARIAN COMMUNITY.

NO existing Community has had a sadder history than Icaria. That in face of all the obstacles that have confronted them the Icarians should have held together so long and accomplished so much is a marvel. Follow their history as told by President Sauva in a sketch published in the AMERICAN SOCIALIST:

Their founder, Etienne Cabet, was born at Dijon in France in 1788, and before he appeared in the *role* of a social theorist had made a name as a politician, editor and historical writer. His *Voyage en Icarie*—an imaginary work descriptive of life in a happy land of Communism—was published in 1840, and at once made him a recognized leader among French Social ists. He soon after commenced the journal *Le Populaire*, to advocate his principles, and erelong had an immense following. In 1847 there were hundreds of thousands of Icarian Communists. They abounded, not alone in France, but in Switzerland, Spain, Germany, England, and even in South America. Cabet was not content with the dissemination of his principles. He determined to experiment in practical Communism, and for this purpose made preparations for the settlement of a large colony in the United States. He secured for this purpose one million of acres in the State of Texas, and called on his disciples to help him establish Icaria. "The effect of this call was indescribable. Thousands of congratulations came to him from all parts. His scheme became the topic for all the journalists. Some supported it, others denounced or ridiculed it, but the greater number favored it.

"Thousands of Icarians claimed the honor of being the first colonists. Assisted by a committee appointed by the Paris Icarians, Cabet took all the necessary measures, made all the preparations, selected sixty-nine of his most devoted disciples, all young and stout men, able to stand the fatigues and privations which awaited them; and on the 3d of February, 1848, this first vanguard left France, sailed for the United States, carrying with them the best wishes and encouragements of hundreds of thousands of Communists. How strange is destiny! Three weeks later, the departure of the first Icarians for America would probably not have taken place; and the realization of Icaria would probably be yet future. Neither Cabet nor his school had foreseen that twenty-one days after the departure of the first company the Republic would be proclaimed in Paris.

"The revolution which took place on the 24th of February, 1848, was the first, and, according to our notion, the most severe check experienced by the Icarian undertaking. The Icarian school, which had been so well united until that time, became divided. Some were in favor of recalling the first departure, of giving up the idea of emigration, and of devoting themselves exclusively to the success of the new Republic. Others, with a better appreciation of the events, sided with Cabet, and were willing to continue the work, foreseeing that nothing good could be expected from a revolution at the head of which were such men as Lamartine, Ledru Rollin, Marie, Marrast and other republicans of that shade, whose hostility against all social reforms was notorious. But the first blow was struck, the union was broken. Cabet himself was hesitating between two preöccupations which neutralized his energy. It was for him a terrible moment. In the meanwhile the advance-guard, arriving at New Orleans toward the end of March, learned that a Republic was proclaimed in France. The most bitter regrets manifested themselves among them. The motion to return to France was made, but it did not prevail, and the pioneers of the great Icarian Community proceeded toward the place selected for their settlement.

"Toward the month of June, 1848, they laid the foundations of the Iarian Colony in Fanin Co., Texas.

"They built a few miserable huts, undertook to break prairie, but they were soon stopped in their work by the malaria, which assailed and demoralized them, depriving them of the only physician they had, Doctor Roveira, who became insane, besides five of their number who died; and the others were compelled to abandon the place.

"This abandonment was a bitter disappointment to the first vanguard, and it was not without regret that they made up their minds to retreat. They left on the place five of their brethren: Guillot, Collet, Guérin, Chauvin and Saugé. They started back toward Shreveport and New Orleans, where they hoped to meet other Icarians who were coming to join them. There stood before them a distance of from three to five hundred miles to travel through a lonely country, without any resources, and laboring under sickness. The retreat from Texas was one of the most saddening events in the Icarian enterprise. For fear of not finding on the same route the necessary supplies for such a company, the Icarians divided themselves into three equal squads, and dragged themselves toward their rendezvous. These squads disbanded themselves on the road; sickness prevented several from following their friends. Four of them died from exertion and privations. The remnant of this first vanguard, together with a few members of the second vanguard whom they met on the road, arrived finally at New Orleans toward the end of 1848.

"In the meanwhile other departures had been effected from France. Cabet himself, left Paris in December, and in March,

1849, the Icarians, numbering 280, with their leader at their head, left New Orleans and went to establish themselves at Nauvoo, Illinois. This was a good place for a temporary settlement. Houses were plenty. By the departure of Joseph Smith's followers the population of Nauvoo had been reduced from fifteen or twenty thousand inhabitants to three or four thousand.

"Cabet and his followers settled there. From 1850 to 1855 many new members came to augment their number. The colony became prosperous. They had work-shops, farms, a flouring-mill and a distillery. They had a school for their children, and published a newspaper. From time to time they issued pamphlets to propagate their principles. They had an office in Paris and correspondents every-where.

"The colony being mostly composed of French people, amusements were not forgotten. They had a theater with Icarian artists. They organized a musical band of about fifty instruments.

"In 1855 the colony numbered five hundred members.

"Convinced that Nauvoo was only a temporary settlement, and that the great Community was to be established in some other locality, the Icarians in 1853 purchased three thousand acres of land in Iowa. A few pioneers were sent to prepare for the future transfer of the Community.

"Until then Cabet's moral authority over his followers did not seem to have been lessened. He was the leader and the honored father of the Icarian family.

"But most of the Icarians had been former revolutionists. The authority of the founder of Icaria, however mild, reasonable and legitimate it might be, became by degrees a burden to them; they had submitted to it because they believed it indispensable to the success of the undertaking, but they now thought the time had come to free themselves from it.

"Cabet was getting old. His intellectual faculties were declining, and a secret conspiracy against his authority had been forming for some time.

"The war broke out.

"Suffice it to say, that after a pacific though grievous struggle, which lasted over a year, a strong minority of about two hundred members left Nauvoo with Cabet at their head. The old champion of the great humanitarian cause was annihilated. He had dared every thing during his long career: criticism, insult, calumny. provocation, imprisonment, exile. Nothing affected him so much as the deplorable events which now occurred.

"Cabet was sixty-nine years old. On the 8th of November, 1856, he died in a fit of apoplexy, in St. Louis, Missouri. The death of Cabet was a terrible blow for those who followed him. Many of them lost all hope of continuing their undertaking and abandoned their brethren, who, having a stronger faith and enthusiasm in their belief, devoted themselves with a greater courage to accomplish his work.

"They settled within a few miles of St. Louis, and started the Cheltenham Community. They enjoyed a moment of apparent prosperity, but reverses assailed them. Sickness, poverty, division, decimated the colony.

"Still the few persevering ones who had remained would not have surrendered themselves if financial embarrassments had not compelled them to do so. But such heroism was useless. The claws of their creditors sank deeper every day in the throat of the unfortunate victim, and in January, 1864, the Cheltenham Community expired. Thus ended one of the branches of the Icarian Community. The other one, established at Nauvoo, remained there until 1859, when those who had resolved to continue the work, wishing to show that they could live and grow without being under the rule of their founder, retired to their Iowa colony.

"New trials awaited them in this place. Uncertainty as to their future prospects, want and poverty, were their share for many years.

"The amount of devotedness, confidence in their principles, and perseverance required by the Icarians of the first hour, to go through all the stages of Icarian history, will never be known.

"Now Icaria is free from material embarrassment. Without being in a very prosperous condition, it stands upon a solid basis. Its fidelity to the great principle of human fraternity has not failed. Now, as well as on the first day of its existence, it believes in and proclaims equality of rights and equality of duties for all the children of Nature. It is opposed to every idea of superiority, whether based upon muscular strength, intellect or wealth. It does not make any distinction between the son of a poor man and the son of a king. In its estimation all are equal, all have a right to receive from society the entire satisfaction of their wants, all have the duty to produce according to the amount of strength with which they are endowed by Nature. Such is Icaria."

———

In the summer of 1876 the author visited Icaria, and thence wrote the following letter to the AMERICAN SOCIALIST:

"*Corning, Adams Co., Iowa, Aug.* 14, 1876.

"A dozen small white cottages arranged on the sides of a parallelogram; a larger central building, containing a unitary kitchen and a common dining-hall, which is also used as an assembly-room and for Community amusements, including an occasional dance or theatrical presentation; a unitary bake-room and laundry near at hand; numerous log-cabins, also within easy reach of the central building—forcible reminders of the early poverty and hardships of this people; a small dairy-house near the thatched stable to the south; bains for the horses and sheep to the north: all these buildings on the bluff rising from the valley of the Nodaway river, and surrounded by the Community domain of over two thousand acres of fertile land, of which seven hundred have been cultivated, and including, with some timber-land, extensive meadows and pastures, over which range 600 sheep and 140 head of cattle—the cultivated part having the present season 5 acres of potatoes, 5 acres of sorghum, 100 of wheat, 250 of corn, 1 1-2 of strawberries, besides vineyards, orchards, etc.: behold the present external aspects of Icaria.

"At the sound of the bell all direct their footsteps to the central building; and should you enter at meal-time you would see the entire Community, now numbering seventy-five, seated at the oblong and circular tables, as lively and sociable as French people know how to be. Over the entrance-door you would notice in large letters the word 'Equality,' and directly opposite the word 'Liberty,' and at one end of the room the suggestive "1776—1876." You would notice also that upon the table there is a great abundance of substantial food, but that every thing is plain.

"Should you enter the same building at evening you might find most of the family assembled, some to dance, some to converse, some to sing their songs of equality and fraternity. Or should your call be on a Sunday afternoon, as was my good fortune, you might hear selections from the writings of their great apostle, Etienne Cabet, or recitals by the young, or songs, perchance, which would stir your Socialistic enthusiasm. One of those I heard had this refrain:

'Travaillers de la grande cause,
Soyons fiers de notre destin;
L'égoiste seul se repose,
Travaillons pour le genre humain.'

"A recital by a maiden of fifteen was very effective. She put great expression into the words:

> ' Mes frères, il est temps que les haines s'oublient ;
> Que sous un seul drapeau les peuples se rallient ;
> Le chemin du salut va pour nous s'aplanir.
> La grande liberté que l'Humanité rêve,
> Comme un nouveau soleil, radieuse, se lève
> Sur l'horizon de l'avenir.'

"It is indeed time that hatreds were forgotten and that all people rallied under a single flag. Shall that flag be Communism? The Icarians will enthusiastically answer, 'Yes;' and yet should one inquire whether all hatreds are forgotten in Icaria itself, would the reply be also 'Yes?'

"Icaria has existed for twenty-nine years. It has overcome the hardships and endured the severe privations inseparably connected with the upbuilding of a Community in a new country and without capital. It commenced in poverty. It now has $60,000 in real and personal property, encumbered only with a debt of about $4,000. Its numbers are more than double what they were eight or ten years ago. It is building every year additional houses for the better accommodation of its members. It is setting out orchards and vineyards, and beginning the cultivation of small fruits. It is talking about radical improvements as though it expected to realize them in the near future. It is anticipating an increase of numbers, and lately received four families. And though it offers few attractions, having no facilities for a higher education or esthetic culture, and is destitute of some of the comforts and many of the conveniences of communal life, I still see no reason why it may not attain permanent success provided *it has sufficient power of agreement.*

"The experiment here is an attempt to form a prosperous Community without religion, or perhaps we should express the Icarian idea better by saying, without Christ

and the Bible and theology. If it succeeds the Icarians
will be entitled to the greatest praise. To build a Community is like building a brick house—the better the cement
or mortar the stronger the walls. It has been demonstrated
that with a strong religious afflatus it is possible to make
good mortar. The Icarians are confident that they can make
mortar suitable for laying up high walls, with the principles
of equality, liberty and fraternity. *Nous verrons.*

"Some of the Icarian principles will be more severely
tested when their numbers have increased. Their system is
founded on pure democracy, with its unrestricted free discussion. Such discussion may be allowed in a small Community,
but might it not become unbearable in a large one? And
then no Community organization should be at the mercy of a
majority. If mere numbers carry the day, as is the case in
Icaria, it is possible that the most worthy in a Community
may have the least power. Woe be to the Community
in that condition. It might have been better had it not
been born.

"As I have previously remarked in my letters to the
AMERICAN SOCIALIST, one of the most vital questions concerned
in successful Communism is this: How should individual liberty and subordination to the central power of a Community
stand related to each other? The principle of subordination
may be so magnified as to seriously interfere with the proper
development of the individual members, and, on the other
hand, individualism may assert its claims so strongly as to
endanger the governmental power of the Community. If the
Inspirationists, Harmonists and other Communists stand at
one extreme in this respect, the Icarians are at the other.
The true mean will be discovered when a way is found to
secure perfect obedience to the central principle of the organization, and at the same time make the individual free to de-

velop, fully and naturally, all the powers with which he is created.

"One cannot withhold his admiration from the little band at Icaria—a mere remnant of the army assembled at Nauvoo under Cabet. Of every half-score that could then have responded to the roll-call scarcely one is left; and yet they are apparently as full of courage and as enthusiastically devoted to Communism as they would have been had their pathway been strewn with roses instead of beset with thorns.

"W. A. H."

The following questions and answers will convey to the reader definite information on some additional points pertaining to this interesting Community. It is proper to mention that the answers were given last September by President Sauva:

"What is the present population of Icaria?"

"Eighty-three."

"Have you many applications for membership?"

"We have on hand fifty applications."

"How many members have been received the past year?"

"Seventeen definitely and three provisionally."

"What are your rules respecting the admission of new members?"

"An applicant can be received, can be allowed to pass a novitiate of six months, and be definitely admitted as a member of the Community, only on the concurrence of three-fourths of the voting members."

"Do you desire a large increase of members?"

"Certainly. It is both our duty and our interest; but our means and the difficulty of finding suitable material have prevented a very rapid growth."

"What businesses do you rely on for your income?"

"Besides a saw- and grist-mill run by steam-power, we rely upon the cultivation of our land and the increase of our herds and flocks."

"How much land have you? and what proportion of it is under cultivation?"

"We have 2,150 acres. 700 are now under cultivation; 400 are covered with timber; the rest is prairie pasture."

"How much stock have you?"

"We have between 30 and 40 horses, 140 head of cattle, and 600 sheep."

"Has your Community been prosperous, financially and otherwise, the past year?"

"The last two years have not been financially favorable to Icaria; our harvests have been poor, and we still feel the consequences."

"Your system, as I understand it, is theoretically one of pure Communism in property. Is this idea fully realized in your practical life?"

"Our system, as you say, contemplates Communism of goods in all its purity; but we have thus far only imperfectly realized it; but whatever departure there may be from principle in our practice is constantly tending to disappear. No money is furnished to members for their private use."

"Each house, I have noticed, has a small garden. Are the gardens cultivated for the Community or for the benefit of individuals?"

"Every family has a small garden in which it can cultivate flowers and fruits, which are entirely at its disposal; but a considerable part of the Society consider this practice a departure from our principles, and ask for its suppression."

"Your system is also, as I conceive it, one of pure democracy. How far is it found practicable to carry this principle out in daily life?"

"Our system is a pure democracy, and we experience no difficulty in its application."

"Are the officers simply executive, every thing being determined by vote?"

"Our officers are elected to execute the decisions of the General Assembly or legislative body, and have no other power."

"What are the officers of your Society? How are they elected? and for what time?"

"The officers of the Icarian Community are: a Director of Agriculture, a Director of Industry, a Director of Clothing and of Lodging, a Secretary, Treasurer and President. They are elected annually on the 3d of February, by the simple majority of members, and hold their positions always subject to the pleasure of the Community."

"Marriage is said to be obligatory in Icaria: how much is to be understood by this? Does it simply mean that it is expected and desired that all members shall marry? or that no one would be received who should decline to enter into the marriage relation?"

"Marriage is obligatory here; that is to say, celibacy is considered an anomalous condition, contrary to nature, to be tolerated only when the number of members is so limited as to prevent the celibates, men and women, from readily finding suitable mates."

"What are your means of discipline? How would you deal with any transgressor of the Society's regulations, or with any offender against morality and good order?"

"Transgressions of the principles, laws and regulations of the Community are punished by public censure, by deprivation of civil rights, or by the exclusion of the transgressors, according to the gravity of the offenses."

"How are the occupations of members determined?"

"By individual preferences and by the requirements of labor."

"What is the position of women in Icaria? Have they any voice or vote in the business meetings?"

"They come to the assemblies; they take part in the deliberations; they are at liberty to make propositions, and to discuss those made by others; they can offer their opinion and counsel, but are not permitted to vote."

"Am I right in supposing you exalt the principles of Communism into religion—considering that they do essentially embody religion or Christianity?"

"You are perfectly right in supposing that we elevate the principle of Communism, and especially the principle of fraternity, into the place of religion; but Christianity in its primitive purity is held with us in great esteem; and of personal opinion in matters of religion there is in Icaria the greatest tolerance, provided its expression does not result in trouble and disorder to the Community."

The statement of President Sauva, that there has been no difficulty in the practical application of the Icarian system of pure democracy, conveys an idea of harmony that is scarcely consonant with the facts; but he may have simply intended to say the businesses of the Community had been successfully conducted. However that may be, it is certain that for some time there has been a growing tendency toward the formation of two distinct and even antagonistic parties in Icaria. Previous to the author's visit to the Community in the summer of 1876 there had been a serious altercation between these parties, which had however terminated amicably; for which reason he deemed it inexpedient to publicly call attention to the matter at the time. But the harmony resulting from the compromise measures then adopted was superficial and illusory; the old antagonisms soon began to reässert themselves, and at the present time there appears to be an irreparable breach between the two parties; one of which is cautious, prudent, and averse to radical changes, preferring to "hasten slowly" as in the past; while the other considers that the time has arrived for making many improvements in the practical life of the Community, for multiplying its industries, improving its educational conditions, giving the ballot to *les Icariennes,* etc. etc. The first includes mainly the older members of the Community; the second, many of the young men and women who have grown up in the Community, recently-received members and others; and though comprising a numerical majority includes a minority of voters; the Icarian Constitution prescribing that only males above twenty years of age shall be permitted to cast the ballot.

The second party having made several propositions to amend the Constitution which were rejected by the General Assembly, finally proposed terms of separation. They asked:

" That a division of land and stock be made *pro-rata,* each stockholder, man, woman and child, to be given ten acres of land; that henceforth we carry on our affairs, agricultural, industrial and financial, as two distinct branches of one Community; that the land be held on both sides in usufruct only, each branch having the privilege of mortgaging its land to one-fifth of its appraised valuation; that each branch admit to its ranks such new members as it may deem proper (births being reckoned as new admissions); and that the surplus of land remaining, after the division shall be made according to the above proposition, shall be held in common at the disposal of both sides for the use of its new members. In case of death on either side, if the portion held in the name of the deceased is not taken up by a new admission within a specified time, the opposite party shall have the right to claim it."

This proposition having also been rejected by the majority of voters, the "young party" have taken extra-constitutional measures to effect a separation.

It appears from the testimony of both sides that there is no lack of zeal for Communism. All are ready to live and die for that. The irreconcilable difference is over a question of Community policy. Should the Community be severed in twain, each part would become a distinct Community and endeavor to realize its social ideal.

A recent visitor at Icaria, in a letter to the *Corning Union,* written after a ten-days' sojourn in the Community, says:

"The Community of Icaria is but a miniature republic, with its elaborate Constitution, its laws, rules and regulations, its President and civil authorities, its politicians, office-seekers, and its assemblies; and it is subject to all the conditions, variations and changes of any other republic. A republic cannot exist without party, and this word is the key to the 'Trouble in Icaria;' trouble expanded to such an extent that the Community has been shaken as if by an earthquake, until the machinery of its internal organization, its laws, rules and regulations have ceased to work. There has been a struggle between a progressive and a conservative party here, as in all governments, and who would have it otherwise? Is not progressiveness a check upon the bigotry of extreme conservatism? And is not conservatism a check upon the empiricism of extreme progressiveness? Is it not to this conflict that humanity owes every thing it owns and nearly all it knows?"

This may be a wise view of the matter; but it is certainly conceivable that even a republic might have unexampled prosperity under one party. Indeed, the people of the United States point to the one-party episode in its history, during President Monroe's administration, as a kind of political millennium. But leaving the question of politics,

it is certain that Communities *must* find ways to secure unanimity and harmonious action; otherwise the larger they become the less desirable they will be as places of abode. A
religious afflatus can make hundreds, yea thousands, of "one
heart and of one mind;" a capable leader, ruling by truth
and love, may do much to secure the desired unity; but it
is yet to be proved that pure democracy, with its party antagonisms, can hold a large number of persons together in the
close relations of Communism.

The party at Icaria which demands separation say they
have "arrived at the conclusion that they can no longer
live in peace and harmony with the old people;" and
from general observation among the Communities I feel
justified in affirming that the harmonious adjustment of the
relations of the old and young is one of the most difficult
problems which Communities have to solve. In common
society, when a man arrives at the age of twenty-one he becomes legally independent, and is at liberty to choose his own
course in life, and generally leaves the parental roof and
sets up for himself in business, politics and religion. Not so
in Communities. At Icaria the young men become voters at
twenty, but in most of the Communities no change takes
place in the status of the members when they arrive at legal
maturity. They can only hope to fill places of honor as they,
by long courses of faithfulness, commend themselves to all as
persons who can be fully trusted with important interests. If,
on the other hand, the elders have come to love their responsibilities, and to feel that they cannot possibly be as safe in
younger hands as they are in theirs, as is natural, it is obvious
that the process of transferring the interests of a Community
from one generation to another, which always has to be done
sooner or later, will be at least a painful one. The highest
wisdom is needed to make this transfer, and not mar the har-

mony of the Society. Not alone are business and official interests concerned; the transfer may involve questions of policy that seem vital; for each succeeding generation brings with it new truths, which are very likely to give a slight shock even to those who in younger days were themselves radicals and innovators. Happy is the Community whose elders, free from self-seeking, have wisdom to discern when the best interest of the Community requires that they should transfer their official cares to others; and have grace to do it. All this is not applicable to the Icarian Community, where every thing is determined by ballot, and any man over twenty can hold any office to which he is elected. But it is evident that in such a Community, if the party in the majority fails to command the respect and confidence of the minority, there will be evil-thinking and evil-doing that will destroy the general peace and make a state of society more resembling pandemonium than heaven. At Icaria each party thinks the other the cause of all the difficulties which encompass the Community; it is probable that neither party is wholly right nor wholly wrong, and that a wave of the Good Spirit would obliterate all lines of separation and make of the Community one party, that, avoiding all extremes, and combining the wisdom of prudence with the wisdom of progress, would realize the highest destiny. There are noble men and women in Icaria, and for their sakes, and for the sake of the cause for which they have labored so long and endured so much, it is to be hoped that the Icarians will throw to the dogs their bones of contention, send home their lawyers, and strive anew for the harmony which ensures every blessing to communal life.

One of the saddest phases of the Icarian strife is, that it has made enemies of the same household, setting wife against husband and children against parents, and widely sundered ties that should have grown stronger with each succeeding

year. The dissolution of a Community is as much more serious
than the dissolution of a common family as its numbers are
greater and its social and business interests are more complicated. Hence the exceeding importance of careful selection
of material in the formation of Communities. Hence, also,
the imperative obligation resting on every member to strive
for unity and peace. The difficulty of satisfactorily and justly
dividing the property of a Community is an additional induce-
ment to the same end. The proposition of the "young party"
at Icaria, for example, to divide the property *pro-rata*, seems
fair at first glance ; but what if one party includes the greater
number of those who have grown old in the service of the
Community, and those who are enfeebled by disease contracted in such service, while the other party includes most of those
who have been only a few years connected with the Community? It is apparent that in such a case the proposed conditions of separation might work great injustice. And probably
any conditions that might be proposed by either side would in
their application fail to secure exact justice. It is not at all
likely that the lawyers and courts would succeed any better.
And indeed if Communities must dissolve from time to time,
as well as other organizations, they ought to find ways to get
along without resort to force or litigation. Far better would
it be to refer the whole matter to arbitrators, all obligating
themselves to abide by the decision. Better still to divide
their property themselves in the spirit manifested by the
founder of the Putney Community, who, when the Society
seemed on the eve of dissolution in consequence of external
pressure, said: "*If a division of property is necessary to
satisfy our enemies, I shall not be satisfied to have it done on
worldly, selfish principles, or merely according to legal rights,
but on the principle that the strong shall help the weak.*" To
appreciate the noble spirit which prompted these words it is

necessary to understand that the founder of the Putney Community and his wife contributed one-half of its capital, and that many of its members brought in no property.   The spirit which can give such counsel in such circumstances will attract and hold hearts, and form Communities that will withstand all the pressure that can be brought to bear upon them both from within and from without.

THE SHAKERS.

THE Shakers have seventeen Societies, and a total member-ship of about 2,400. Each Society is divided into two or more Families, which are in respect to property and other matters distinct from one another ; so that there may be said to be fifty-seven different Shaker Communities, or fifty-eight if we include the Family of twenty colored persons in Philadelphia.

The Shakers first landed in the United States on the sixth of August, 1774; the first settlement was commenced at Watervliet in 1776; the first completed Community was Mt. Lebanon, which began its organization in 1787. Previous to 1792 two Societies had been formed in New York, four in Massachusetts, one in Connecticut, two in New Hampshire, and two in Maine. Between 1805 and 1807 two Societies were formed in Ohio, one in Indiana, and two in Kentucky. Between 1822 and 1827 two Societies were formed in Ohio, and one in New York. The Indiana Society was broken up on account of unhealthy climatic conditions, and the Tyringham Society of Massachusetts more recently and for other causes.

These Societies had at one time a population of more than double their present number, reaching an aggregate of between five and six thousand souls. The largest Society is Mount Lebanon, with a membership of about 375. Watervliet, N. Y., Union Village, Ohio, and Pleasant Hill and South Union, Ky., have each between two and three hundred members. Watervliet, O., Groveland, N. Y., and Shirley, Mass., are the smallest, having only about fifty members each.

They all have large home farms, ranging from one thou-

sand acres upward, and many of them own additional tracts of
land in the Western and Southern States.   A single Family of
one of the New York Societies a few years ago bought thirty
thousand acres in Kentucky.   It is not easy to ascertain their
aggregate landed estate; but it must nearly or quite reach
one hundred thousand acres.   They give as reasons for not
making public the acreage of the Societies, that they "own too
much land," "more than they can profitably pay taxes on."
They were long under the land-mania, and "bought all that
joined them" and a great deal that did not join them.   The
wiser heads among them now regret their past policy in this
respect.   They find themselves burdened with investments
that yield small returns, and call themselves "land poor."
It is impossible for them to cultivate their entire domains.
They let land run to forest, selling the wood and timber, as
in some of the Eastern States; make sheep-walks of large
tracts, as at Mt. Lebanon; rent farms, or employ hirelings to
carry them on.   But in no case do they get large returns from
the land when cultivated for ordinary farm purposes; often the
remuneration is very small.   The case is different when they
can raise garden crops, seeds, medicinal herbs, etc., and market
the same without encountering too fierce competition.   I have
been repeatedly told that some simple branch of manufacture,
employing only a few hands, gives more satisfactory returns
than large tracts of farm land, especially when cultivated by
hireling labor.

The raising of garden seeds and medicinal herbs has been
carried on by most of the Shaker Societies, and has been a
principal source of their wealth; but they have also been engaged in several mechanical industries.   They still manufacture brooms and measures, pails and tubs, chairs and mops,
mats and sieves, washing-machines and chimney-caps, and I
know not how many other things.   They put up a variety of

vegetable extracts, and preserve corn, tomatoes, peaches and other vegetables and fruits. And their reputation for good work and honest dealing is proverbial.

Of the wealth of the Shaker Societies it is impossible to speak with definiteness. Nordhoff estimated the wealth of all the American Communities at twelve millions. I have reason to believe that the wealth of the Shaker Societies alone approximates this amount. But whatever property they possess is the reward of faithful industry and economy; and if for any reason they prefer not to make known their exact riches we may well content ourselves with the general fact, that their Communism of property and labor has proved highly favorable to financial prosperity.

The Shaker villages are generally pleasantly located, and with few exceptions have a neat and thrifty look. Their houses and fences are kept in good repair, and every thing is in strictest order. Dixon's picture of Mt. Lebanon is a picture of nearly every Shaker settlement from Maine to Kentucky: "No Dutch town has a neater aspect, no Moravian hamlet a softer hush. The streets are quiet; for here you have no grog-shop, no beer-house, no lock-up, no pound; of the dozen edifices rising about you—work-rooms, bains, tabernacles, stables, kitchens, schools, and dormitories—not one is either foul or noisy; and every building, whatever may be its use, has something of the air of a chapel. The paint is all fresh; the planks are all bright; the windows are all clean. A white sheen is on every thing; a happy quiet reigns around."

Of the origin and early history of the Shakers the briefest statement will suffice. In the early part of the eighteenth century arose the "French prophets," the "Spiritualists" of that early day. They were subject to most remarkable manifestations, which in many respects were like those experienced by modern "mediums." They had visions and revelations, were entranced, spoke with eloquent power under spiritual control, and were also subject to violent agitations of the body. The movement of which the "French prophets" were the center soon extended to other countries, and in England spread far and wide. In 1747 some members of the Society of Quakers, who had become subjects of this spirit-ualistic revival, formed themselves into a society of which Jane and James Wardley were the leaders. The members were often in their meetings seized with a mighty trembling; at other times they sang their songs of praise, shouting and leaping for joy; sometimes they would be compelled to shake their limbs, or run, or walk, "with a variety of other operations and signs, swiftly passing and repassing each other, like clouds agitated with a mighty wind."* These strange exercises gave them the appellation of *Shakers*, which they have since borne. Of course persecution followed, which only increased their numbers and unity. Ann Lee joined them with her parents, and soon became a prominent member, and in 1770, while in prison, professed to have had a great revelation of Christ's kingdom and glory, of man's loss and the way of redemption, accompanied with a flow of the power of God into her soul which was like a fountain of living water. From that time she was acknowledged as Mother in Christ and called *Mother Ann;* and from that time she was "able to take up a full cross against all the doleful works of the flesh," and especially against the great sin which caused the fall of Adam.

Four years later she received a revelation directing her to come to America, where the true Christian Church would be established—a revelation accompanied by such "signs, visions, and extraordinary manifestations" as left no room for doubts. Eight believers accompanied her, including her husband,

---

* " Shaker Compendium," pp. 18-22.

who apostatized soon after their arrival in this country. The captain of the vessel on which they made the passage across the Atlantic forbade their peculiar demonstrations on board; but they, fearing God rather than man, went forth in the dance with songs and shoutings. The captain was enraged, threatened to put them overboard, and actually proceeded to carry out his threat, when, a plank starting, the ship sprung a leak, and he was glad of their assistance at the pumps. They were in great peril, but Mother Ann maintained her confidence in God, and said: "Captain, be of good cheer; there shall not a hair of our heads perish; we shall all arrive safe in America." Shortly after, a wave struck the ship with great violence and closed the plank into its place, which wonderful circumstance was viewed by all on board as nothing less than a miraculous interposition of Providence.

Arriving in New York August, 1774, Mother Ann remained there for nearly two years, while most of her companions went up the river to Albany; but all were dependent for support on the labor of their hands, and Mother Ann sought employment as a washer-woman.

In 1776 a settlement was made at Niskayuna, seven miles from Albany. There they quietly remained, subduing the wilderness and the flesh, until, four years later, they were called, as they believe by a divine voice, to proclaim the millennial gospel to the world.

A great revival of religion occurred at New Lebanon and in towns adjacent. The people were painfully and wonderfully exercised in body and soul. In their meetings loud cries were heard for the Kingdom to come, and a powerful testimony was given against all sin. Some cried for mercy; others felt unspeakably happy. But the work was short, and when the Spirit was withdrawn many were plunged in deep distress, while still earnestly praying for the advent of Christ's Kingdom. Finally, in 1780, some of those who had been engaged in the revival visited Mother Ann, and were immediately convinced that she and her followers were "in the very work for which they themselves had been so earnestly praying." Others soon visited the Shakers, and their fame was spread abroad. Persecution followed. Mother Ann and her disciples were accused of treason, and several of them, including Mother Ann herself, imprisoned; and this in turn made them more widely known.

After her release, accompanied by five of her disciples she made a journey to Massachusetts and Connecticut, which has been described as "a triumphal tour and a march to the cross." They were gone two years, and proclaimed the testimony to many thousands who thronged to hear them, but they suffered all manner of trials, and were repeatedly in danger of losing their lives.

In 1784 Mother Ann died, in the forty-ninth year of her age. She was succeeded in the ministry by Elder James Whittaker, and he shortly by Elder Joseph Meacham, of American birth and the great organizer of Shaker Communities. Of the system which he introduced and its present working, as well as of the general objects and principles of Shakerism, I prefer to let the Shakers speak for themselves; and the quoted paragraphs that immediately follow are taken directly from their published works:

THE PRINCIPLES OF SHAKERISM.

The Shaker Church rests upon a foundation of four "pillars, or basic principles; these are *Virgin Purity* and *Christian Communism; Confession of Sin*, and *Separation from the World.*

" *Virgin Purity* is of the utmost consequence in the Shaker Life. To secure this, *Confession of Sin* is essential, because all have sinned in a greater or less degree; and sin of any kind defiles the spirit. Hence, to live in purity we must first become pure, by removing all that defiles in thought, word and deed. In other words, whatever is contrary to the pure Christ spirit or virgin character must be brought to the light, and confession made thereof to God in the presence of a confidential witness.

"*Christian Communism*, which may be shown to be rational, and is certainly scriptural, follows as a sequence. The bond of union which unites all Shakers is spiritual and religious, hence unselfish. All are equal before God and one another; and, as in the institution of the primitive Christian Church, all share one interest in spiritual and temporal blessings, according to individual needs;—no rich, no poor. The strong bear the infirmities of the weak, and all are sustained, promoting each other in Christian fellowship, as one family of brethren and sisters in Christ, acknowledging God the universal Father and Mother, or the principle of Divine parentage.

"But Christian Communism cannot be maintained without a *Separation from the World.* Christian Communism, based upon Virginity, or Purity, with Confession of Sin as a safeguard, implies a total separation from, and antagonism to, all that is worldly or non-Christian. All worldly usages, manners, customs, loves and affections, which interpose between the individual citizen of the heavenly kingdom and his duties and privileges therein, must be abandoned.

"True Christian Communism can exist only through the principle of the Virgin Life. This excludes marriage from Shakerism;—that, being a selfish relation, cannot be incorporated with Communism, and does not belong to the Resurrection order, according to the words of Jesus Christ: 'For in the resurrection, they neither marry nor are given in marriage; but are as the angels of God in heaven.' (Matt. 22: 30.)

"Marriage is not condemned in its order; but that order

is of the earth, earthy, according to the text which reads, 'They twain shall be one flesh'—there is no reference to the spirit in the contract. It belongs to the first Adam, not to the second.

"Jesus lived the virgin life,—left the earthly order to be fulfilled by those who remain on that plane. He is the Shaker exemplar; surely, to live as Jesus lived cannot be wrong.

"He taught that no man was worthy to be called his disciple until he would give up all to follow him,—to live as he lived. And that there might be no mistake about this, we are told that 'all' includes father, mother, wife, children, house and lands; yea, a man's own life also. Thus a perfectly unselfish surrender was the qualification for Christian fellowship.

"The Shakers claim that a life based upon these principles secures salvation from sin and sorrow, produces happiness here, in the present existence, which increases with growth of soul in the life beyond; and that it is the highest type of Christianity as taught by Jesus Christ, and revived by Ann Lee." *

These four principles—

> *Virgin Purity,*
> *Christian Communism,*
> *Confession,*
> *Separation from the World,*—

are put forth as the essential things; but the Shakers have, besides, a very comprehensive theology on such points as

> The Duality of the Godhead,
> Salvation from Sin,
> The Second Appearing of Christ,
> The Resurrection,
> The New Birth,
> The Millennium,
> The Judgment, etc.,

---

* "Brief Account of Shakers and Shakerism."

which are elaborated in large works. It is perhaps sufficient here to say they believe the Deity is male and female; that it is possible to live a sinless life; that the second appearing of Christ (not *Jesus*, whom they regard as only a man) took place in Mother Ann; that there is no resurrection of the body, but a progressive resurrection of the spirit; that the new birth requires the united influence of spiritual parents, in the order of male and female, and as the eternal Christ in Jesus is the male, so the eternal Christ in Mother Ann is the female, constituting the father and mother of all the children of God; that the millennial reign and the final judgment have begun: hence they call themselves the Millennial Church.

For a succinct view of the position of the Shakers I append the following statement prepared at my solicitation by a prominent member of their body:

"Our interpretation of Shakerism is, that it is not only a condemning testimony to the perversions of human passions and the commonly acknowledged *worldly evils*, such as are enumerated in Galatians 5: 19-21, but it denies the practice of much *worldly good* which Judaism recommended, and for which Jesus only expressed admiration. In this latter class may be included marriage, war, retaliations, private property, and many worldly Judaical honors and practices. The Shakers pronounce these all good under Judaism, but very wrong, impossible, for Christians to practice. While marriage and reproduction are excellent institutions under Judaism, virgin celibacy alone is recognized as the possible life of a Christian, and that there never was, nor can be, a child conceived and born under Christian auspices. War is permitted for Jews and heathen, but not even a retaliation for an injury done is admissible under Jesus, but rather in all things giving the kiss for the blow. Following marriage and reproduction, private property for the sustenance of the family was recommended by Judaism; restricted, however, by regulations which allowed none to become inordinately rich while some were made inordinately poor. The gospel of Jesus overtops Judaism by the greater excellence of its principles. It proclaims universal brotherhood, a common interest among all 'who do the will of the Father.' The Shakers have given more cause of offense because of their unwillingness to practice *worldly good* than from any denunciation of *worldly evils.*"

RULES WHICH GOVERN THE ADMISSION OF MEMBERS TO SHAKER SOCIETIES.

" 1. All persons who unite with this Society, in any degree, must do it freely and voluntarily, according to their own faith and unbiased judgment.

" 2. In the testimony of the Society, both public and private, no flattery or any undue influence is used; but the most plain and explicit statements of its faith and principles are laid before the inquirer: so that the whole ground may be comprehended, as far as possible, by every candidate for admission.

" 3. No considerations of property are ever made use of by this Society to induce any person to join it, nor to prevent any person from leaving it.

" 4. No believing husband or wife is allowed, by the principles of this Society, to separate from an unbelieving partner, except by mutual agreement; unless the conduct of the unbeliever be such as to warrant a separation by the laws of God and man. Nor can any husband or wife who has otherwise abandoned his or her partner be received into communion with the Society.

" 5. Any person becoming a member must rectify all his wrongs, and as fast and as far as it is in his power discharge all just and legal claims, whether of creditors or filial heirs. Nor can any person not conforming to this rule long remain in union with the Society. But the Society is not responsible for the debts of individuals before nor after they become members, except by agreement; because such responsibility would involve a principle ruinous to the institution.

"6. It is an established principle in the Society, that children who are faithful and obedient to their parents until they become of age are justly entitled to their equal portion of the estate of their parents, whether they continue with the Society or not.

"7. If an unbelieving wife separate from a believing husband by agreement, the husband must give her a just and reasonable share of the property; and if they have children who have arrived at years of understanding sufficient to judge for themselves, and who choose to go with their mother, they are not to be disinherited on that account."

THE DIFFERENT ORDERS.

The Shaker Societies are divided each into two or more branches, commonly called Families. This division is generally "made for the sake of convenience, and is often rendered necessary on account of local situation and occurrent circumstances; but the proper division and arrangement of the Community, without respect to local situation, is into three Classes, or progressive degrees of Order, as follows:

"The first, or *Novitiate Class*, are those who receive faith, and come into a degree of relation with the Society, but choose to live in their own families, and manage their own temporal concerns. Any who choose may live in this manner, and be owned as brethren and sisters in the gospel, so long as they live up to its requirements.

"Believers of this class are not controlled by the Society, either with regard to their property, children, or families; but act as freely in all these respects as the members of any other religious Society, and still enjoy all their spiritual privileges, and maintain their union with the Society; provided they do not violate the faith, and the moral and religious principles of the institution.

"The second, or *Junior Class*, is composed of persons who, not having the charge of families, and being under no embarrassments to hinder them from uniting together in Community order, choose to enjoy the benefits of that situation. These (for mutual safety) enter into a contract to devote their services freely to support the interest of the Family of which they are members, so long as they continue in that order; stipulating at the same time to claim no pecuniary compensation for their services; and all the members of such Families are mutually benefited by the united interest and labors of the whole Family, so long as they continue to support the order thereof; and they are amply provided for in health, sickness, and old age. These benefits are secured to them by contract.

"Members of this class have the privilege, at their option, by contract, to give freely the improvement of any part or all of their property, to be used for the mutual benefit of the Family to which they belong. The property itself may be resumed at any time, according to the contract; but no interest can be claimed for the use thereof; nor can any member of such Family be employed therein for wages of any kind. Members of this class may retain the lawful ownership of all their own property, as long as they think it proper, and choose so to do; but at any time, after having gained sufficient experience to be able to act deliberately and understandingly, they may, if they choose, dedicate and devote a part, or the whole, and consecrate it forever to the support of the institution. But this is a matter of free choice.

"The third, or *Senior Class*, is composed of such persons as have had sufficient time and opportunity practically to prove the faith and manner of life practiced in the Society, and are thus prepared to enter fully, freely and voluntarily into a united and consecrated interest. These covenant and agree to dedicate and devote themselves and services, with all that they possess, to the service of God and the support of the gospel forever, solemnly promising never to bring debt nor damage, claim nor demand, against the Society, nor against any member thereof, for any property or service which they have thus devoted to the uses and purposes of the institution. This class constitutes what is called the *Church Order*.

"To enter fully into this order is considered by the Society to be a matter of the utmost importance to the parties concerned, and therefore requires the most mature and deliberate consideration; for, after having made such a dedication, according to the laws of justice and equity, there can be no ground for retraction. Nor can they, by those laws, recover any thing whatever which has been thus dedicated. Of this all are fully apprised before entering into the contract. Yet should any afterwards withdraw, the Trustees have discretionary power to bestow upon them whatever may be thought reasonable, not on the ground of any just or legal claim, but merely as an act of charity. No person, however, who withdraws peaceably is sent away empty." *

GOVERNMENT.

"The Ministry, who are the central executive of the whole order, consist of two brethren and two sisters; and every regularly organized Community or Family in a Society have two *elder* brethren and two *elder* sisters, who have the charge of the *spiritual* affairs; also two deacons and two deaconesses, who have the care of the *temporalities*. All

---

* " Brief Exposition of the Established Principles and Regulations of the United Society of Believers."

other positions of care and trust are filled after the same dual order."* The Ministry at Mt. Lebanon is called the Head of Influence, and is sovereign over all the Shaker Communities wherever located. It is composed of four persons, but one of the four is preëminent; the other three are his advisers. He may depose any of them, and may appoint his own successor. The deacons and deaconesses are subordinate to the elders and eldresses, as the latter are to the Ministry. Throughout the whole Society, the inferiors report to the superiors. Authority is transmitted from the head down, and one rank obeys another.

From the presentation already made it will be seen that the Shakers have had able leaders, with clearly defined principles, and that they have elaborated a thorough system of organization. That this system has been effective for nearly a century in holding thousands of people together in unity, and in producing industry, temperance, honesty, and all the common virtues, is known wherever their name has gone in all the world. And who can estimate the value of their example in Christian Communism? As the author of the "History of American Socialisms" has pointed out, the world is more indebted to the Shakers than to all other social architects of modern times; their success having been the " specie basis " that has upheld all the paper theories, and counteracted the failures of the French and English schools. Their example has, indeed, encouraged every effort at Communism in this country and in Europe which has been attempted since the walls of their Zion were laid at Mt. Lebanon in 1787.

Nor have their great successes been achieved without the usual accompaniments of hardships, privations, and persecu-

* " Shaker's Compendium."

tion. We have seen how Mother Ann and her first followers,. after their arrival in this country, labored at menial employments, were imprisoned without cause, and received all manner of personal abuse, and how even their lives were in jeopardy. And after they began their first settlement at Watervliet, New York, they were reduced to great extremities. We are told that they toiled so hard and fared so poorly that they came to look like walking skeletons; that "at one season their breakfast consisted only of a small bowl of milk-porridge for each, and their supper was the same. For dinner, in addition to the bowl of porridge, they had a piece of cake two and a-half inches square. One day two of the brethren went to the river to catch herring, and one of them was so pressed with hunger that he ate, while yet raw, the first two fish he caught! Their house-room was also limited. They had but little convenience for lodging, and were obliged to sleep upon the floor of their apartment. Some few had a blanket to cover them; others had none."

And of persecution, for the first half century of their existence at least, they had their full share, At Lebanon, Ohio, their houses were beset at night; their windows broken; their persons assaulted with clubs and stones; their fences thrown down; cattle were turned into their grain-fields; their fruit-trees cut and mangled; their horses cropped and otherwise disfigured; their barns and stables, containing their stores of hay and grain, burned, as also their place of worship. "Legal prosecutions were instituted upon frivolous pretenses; petitions drawn up, subscribed and laid before the legislature; and finally, to insure success to their measures, subscription papers, accompanied by malicious reports, and enforced by inflammatory speeches, were industriously circulated with a view to raise offenses sufficient to expel the believers from the country." And in fact a body of five hundred armed men, accompanied by a miscellaneous crowd estimated at fifteen hundred, appeared before the principal dwelling of the Shakers, and demanded that the Society should relinquish their principles and practices, mode of worship and manner of living, or quit the country. But the "calm, peaceable, harmless deportment" of the Shakers had such a quieting effect upon the visitors that they finally left without committing any abuse. What wonder that the believers recognized the "mighty hand" in their deliverance!

The Shaker Societies, beginning with Mount Lebanon, have been the fruits of revivals. Upon revivals the Shakers still place their chief reliance for an increase of membership, which shall fill their large homes with new life and give new prosperity to all their enterprises. Their connection with the Kentucky revival was brought about in so singular a manner that I will briefly state the facts as they are recorded in Shaker books. Shortly before her death Mother Ann had said, "The next opening of the Gospel will be in the southwest; it will be at a great distance, and there will be a great work of God." Remembering these words her followers were expectant, and when reports came to them of the revival in progress in the far-off States of Kentucky and Ohio, the Society at Mount Lebanon sent three messengers — John Meacham, Benjamin S. Youngs and Issachar Bates—to open the testimony of salvation and of the second coming. They set out on the first day of January, 1805, and made a foot journey of more than a thousand miles, in obedience to what seemed to them a divine call. Their message was first opened in Kentucky; but their great work really commenced in Ohio. Guided, as they believed, by Providence, they came to the house of Malcham Worley, in the town of Lebanon—a man of wealth and education, who had been a leader in the great revival. Worley received the messengers almost as angels of

God. From this spot the work spread into the neighboring States of Kentucky and Indiana, and resulted in the formation of the several Societies.

The Shakers are Spiritualists, and had "manifestations" in all their Societies, with mediums by the dozen, long before the "Rochester knockings" were heard of. They appear to have received them at first with great credulity, in some cases verily believing their mediums uttered the words of the Lord Jehovah. The more violent spirit-demonstrations left the Societies in 1844, but to this day they hold communion with departed spirits, receiving almost daily "hymns and spiritual songs" from them; but they have learned to "try the spirits."

Intense religious earnestness has been the distinguishing characteristic of the Shakers, as a body, during their entire history; and this fact must be borne in mind in considering the regulations and customs controlling their practical life, some of which are repugnant to common ideas of individual liberty.

It is a rule in all Shaker Societies that the members shall rise simultaneously at the ringing of the bell, which in the summer is at half-past four, and in the winter at five; and that breakfast shall be an hour and a half after rising; dinner at twelve; supper at six, except on Sunday, when the Shakers rise and breakfast half an hour later, dine lightly at twelve, and sup at four.

A large bell always rings a few moments before meal-time. The brothers and sisters eat apart from each other. Entering the dining-room at separate doors they "quietly arrange themselves near their respective places at the table; then all simultaneously kneel in silent thanks for a few moments, then rise and seat themselves noiselessly at table. No talking, laughing, or whispering is allowed while thus partaking of God's blessings. After eating, all rise together at the signal of the first elder, kneel as before, and leave the room as quietly as they entered, going directly to their labor."

A brother and sister must not pass each other upon the stairs.

The brethren and sisters must not visit each other's rooms except to attend "union meetings" or for some errand of business.

A brother and sister must not converse together except in presence of a third party—a rule that does not, however, prevent an occasional word in passing each other.

A male member must obtain the consent of the elder, and a female member of the eldress, before leaving the premises of the Family where he or she lives. Without this consent one cannot go from one Family to another, no matter how short the distance. The Trustee is excepted from this rule, but he must not absent himself from his Family over night without the consent of his elder.

Confession must be made to the elders, not only of one's past life when he joins the Society, but of all subsequent wrong-doing; and "whoever yields enough to the evil tempter to gratify in the least degree the sensual passion, in deed, word, or thought, must confess honestly the same to his elders ere the sun of another day shall set."*

The dress of both males and females must be plain and without ornamentation, and must conform to established rules.

All who are able must labor a certain number of hours daily, and must subordinate their own wishes respecting choice of industries to the general interest of the Society as expressed through its officers.

No one can absent himself from meeting without permission of his superiors.

---

* Hervey Elkins' "Fifteen Years in the Senior Order of the Shakers."

One must submit his amusements and even his reading to the dictation of superiors, who may also, if they choose, inspect all personal correspondence.

But many regulations which were once rigidly enforced have either been modified or dropped altogether. There is less restriction than formerly regarding the use of books published outside of the Societies; more freedom in conversation and fraternal intercourse; the beard may be worn, once strictly forbidden; instrumental music is now heard in nearly every Shaker Community; flowers are in some Families cultivated for their beauty and fragrance; even the dress of the Shakers has undergone important changes. Thirty years ago the following dress regulations, Elkins says, were observed in all the Societies:

"Hats drab, crown 4 1-2 inches high, rim 4 to 5 inches in width, according to the wearer's breadth of shoulders. All woolen garments for winter use, with the exception of pantaloons, shall be of brownish-drab; pantaloons of a reddish-brown or claret; summer vests of a light blue; summer pantaloons striped blue and white. Females' winter-dress, wine colored alapaca, drugget or worsted; capuchins drab; riding-cloaks deep blue; caps white muslin, and bordered with lace, not crimped, but smooth and starched stiff; vandykes of the same material; scarfs, white muslin or white silk; bonnets of a cylindrical, ungula shape, lined with white silk, and furnished with a veil of white lace; shoes high-heeled, similar to those worn by females half a century ago. Summer dress, white muslin or very light striped."

No one would at the present time mistake a Shaker or Shakeress in costume for a Gentile; but the close observer would detect many departures from the old regulation-standard; and these departures are always in the direction of simplicity and good taste. You may be sure a Shaker will never change his dress for the sake of conforming to fashion; if he changes at all it will be because he has fully satisfied himself that the change will be an improvement.

Once "no image or portrait of any thing upon the earth or under the earth" was suffered to exist in any Society. Now photographs are occasionally taken of the members, but this kind of picture-making is not encouraged by the elders, as it might tend to vanity and idolatry.

In matters of diet great modifications have taken place, especially in the Eastern Societies, for which, I think, Elder Evans of Mount Lebanon deserves especial credit. He has labored zealously to leaven the entire Order with hygienic wisdom on the subject of food, ventilation, drainage, etc.; and he enforces his exhortations with the irresistible logic of facts. Since he began to give attention to sanitary conditions in his Family at Mount Lebanon the drug-store has disappeared and sickness become an unusual thing. Pork is not eaten in any of the Societies; and at Lebanon, and I think in some other Societies, a hygienic table is set for those who prefer that their bread and mush should be made of unbolted flour, their food lightly seasoned, and that no meat should be set before them.

Temperance is universally practiced.

Tobacco is used by a few aged members, but is likely to soon disappear from every Shaker settlement.

Some of the Societies are well furnished with bathing facilities, and in one Family that great luxury and health-agent, the Turkish bath, has been recently introduced.

I think, too, that important changes have taken place in the internal character of Shakerism; that its leaders are more liberal and more tolerant than they were a quarter of a century ago; and that they are more ready to see good in other systems, and less prompt to condemn what does not accord with their own. It is also obvious that there is a growing party of progressives among the Shakers—men and women who, while firmly adhering to all that is deemed essential in the system, think it desirable that all non-essentials that stand in the way of genuine progress and culture should be modified or abolished.

It is a common charge against the Shaker system that its regulations and restrictions are unfavorable to individual development. On this point my observation has led me to the following conclusion: The conditions of communal life existing in Shaker Societies do certainly tend to the development of some high qualities of character, such as obedience, resignation, loyalty, earnestness. Moreover, they are favorable to the development of the talents which are exercised in mechanical invention; and the Shakers claim, and apparently with good reason, to have contributed to general society quite a number of its most useful inventions and mechanical improvements, such as the corn broom, tongue-and-groove machinery, cut nails, Babbitt-metal, an improved washing-machine, an improved lathe, a pea-sheller, mowing- and reaping-machines, etc. But, on the other hand, it has appeared to me that the Shaker system tends to produce two distinctly marked classes; and that while one of them—the governing class, which holds the temporal and spiritual keys—has more than an average amount of shrewd good sense and thinking capacity, the other—the governed class, composed of the rank-and-file—does not compare favorably with the first in culture and general intelligence.

Except as revivals occasionally bring them converts, the Shakers have to depend for their members, in great part, upon the unfortunate people who flock to them for homes when they find the struggle for existence too hard for them; and upon orphans and the children of poor people, glad to put their little ones where they will have enough to eat and wear, and be brought up in habits of strict morality. From such material they have to select the most intelligent for the posts of responsibility; and there is necessarily a remnant that need a great deal of governing. The wonder is that under such circumstances they develop so many really superior men and women. But still the question remains whether their system does not make too great a distinction of classes— whether even in a theocratic form of government like that of the Shakers it is not best to so conduct affairs that every one shall feel, not only that he is personally interested in the general prosperity, but that he contributes to it according to the measure of his ability. Among the Shakers, questions relating to business, for instance, are not discussed in general assembly, but among the leaders only, others being subject to consultation at their option. Nordhoff in his work described a departure which had been made at Union Village, Ohio, in this respect. He said that "in the Church Family once a week all the members—male and female, young and old— were gathered to overhaul the accounts of the week and to discuss all the industrial occupations of the Family;" and he added that "these weekly meetings were found to give the younger members a greater interest in the Society." This was a step in the right direction; and I was sorry to learn on visiting Union Village that the weekly meetings had been discontinued. The easiest way to manage a Community is to perfect the machinery of government, and let a few smart persons run it; but it is not the best way to develop the individual members and draw out their enthusiasm.

But if there is a ruling class in Shakerdom, they do not exempt themselves from labor, or play the "nabob" in matters of dress and luxury. The following rule is strictly applied to every member, high or low: "No one who is able to labor can be permitted to live idly upon the labors of others. All, including ministers, elders and deacons, are required to be employed in some manual occupation, according to their several abilities, when not engaged in other necessary duties." The highest officials work with their hands, as well as the members last received into the fold.

I have spoken of the leaders of the Shaker Societies as men and women of superior ability. This is shown by their system of organization and principles, and by their successful administration. It is also shown by their literature, which includes a large number of works; and those who would thoroughly acquaint themselves with Shakerism should at least read the following: "The Shakers' Compendium," by F. W. Evans; "Dunlavy's Manifesto;" "A Summary View of the Millennial Church;" "The Testimony of Christ's Second Appearing." For a few years past the Order have published a monthly paper, its present title being *The Shaker Manifesto*, which is ably edited by Elder George Albert Lomas of the Watervliet Society.

The central Ministry at Mount Lebanon, which, besides having a general oversight of all the Societies, has especial charge of the New York Societies, is now composed of the following persons: Daniel Boler, Giles B. Avery, Eliza Ann Taylor and Polly Reed. Elder Evans and Eldress Antoinette Doolittle, who preside over the North or Receiving Family of the same Society, are better known than the Ministry itself, as they are more often brought prominently before the public. Of the Hancock (Mass.) and Enfield (Conn.) Bishopric, Thomas Damon is first Minister; of Canterbury and Enfield (N. H.), James S. Kaime; of Harvard and Shirley (Mass.), John Whitely; of Alfred and Gloucester (Maine), Otis Sawyer; of Union Village, North Union, Whitewater and Watervliet (Ohio), Wm. Reynolds; of South Union (Ky.), H. L. Eades; of Pleasant Hill (Ky.), Benjamin B. Dunlavy. These are all men of more than average ability; but there are many, very many others, who as thinkers, writers, speakers, and persons of marked capacity, would deservedly stand high in any society.

The women of the Shaker Societies claim to be fully emancipated—to have equal rights with the men in all respects. The Shaker government is dual in all its departments and offices. The women appear to have as much influence and voice as the men; a woman founded the organization, and a woman held its first office for twenty-five years during its greatest period of prosperity; women are as free as men to speak in their meetings; women are as free as men to write for their paper; women manage their own departments of industry independently of the men.

The Shakers themselves are persuaded that the celibate condition is superior to any other and raises them above the worldly or generative plane. That every human passion may be exercised in the spirit of purity they have not yet learned; and we must respect their earnest efforts to separate themselves from every fleshly temptation that they may lead sinless lives. It is proper to repeat in this connection that they do not wholly condemn marriage, as many people suppose, but, on the contrary, admit that it is a natural and proper relation for those who have not been called to the higher or resurrection order. Their position respecting both marriage and celibacy is well described by H. L. Eades, the able Minister of the South Union Society of Kentucky, when he says: "We Shakers are up-stairs, above the rudimental state of man, which is the generative. The other Communities are down-stairs—still in the rudimental. We are not of that group. Our work is chiefly for the soul and in the soul-world, all externals being merely incidental, whether there are many or few at any given point in space. Theirs is mainly

for the body combined with the intellect; they labor for
their special improvement, comfort, gratification and pleasure
All well enough on the lower (not the lowest) floor, but
whereon no one can be a Christian, because Christ was not
there; while these things with us are ignored or held in
abeyance to the spirit-dictation, in obedience to the teaching
and example of Christ." The Shakers, according to Elder
Eades, recognize three conditions or three stories—the second
floor, first floor, and basement or "lowest floor;" and that it
is all right for those who occupy the first floor to multiply
their kind, but not right for those living in the basement,
because they are too degraded in body and mind; and not right
for those living up-stairs or on the second floor, because they
have been called to flee from the flesh with all its affections
and lusts. Now it is conceivable that the house should have
more than two stories and a basement; that there should be
at least a third story, in which love and parentage are exercised without sensuality or idolatry, and in the spirit of true
science for the good of humanity. If the Shakers could
recognize the truth that the exercise of any function in the
spirit of purity is not only better than its exercise in sensuality, but better than its *disuse*, they might find themselves
going up-stairs again!

Celibacy is thought by many to be less favorable to health
than marriage. If this be true it only proves that the general
conditions of Communism are greatly superior to those of
common society, for the Shakers are unusally long-lived even
for Communists. The eightieth year is often reached, and
some live far past the ninetieth.

But celibacy, as illustrated in the Shaker Societies, is
expensive and uneconomical in many respects. It necessitates
many and large buildings. There must be rooms for the
brothers to occupy before their meals, and similar rooms for

the sisters; there must be an assembly-room at each Family large enough for their marching exercises in worship, with brothers' and sisters' retiring-rooms adjoining; there must be smaller rooms for "union meetings;" there must be sisters' work-rooms; there must be commodious private rooms for the members; there must be separate work-shops for the brothers and the sisters; there must be a church where the different Families constituting a Society can assemble for worship; and so on. Of course the burden of taking care of the buildings falls more heavily on the sisters at the present time than formerly; for the Societies have nearly or quite as many buildings as they had when their present membership was doubled, and they had fewer disabled from active service. Occasionally a Family is given up and the care of a half-score or score of buildings saved. (*Moral to new Communities:* Think long before increasing the number of your buildings; for every addition, beyond the necessities of comfort and health, not only ties up your capital, but lessens your power of productive industry.)

Celibacy places the Shakers at a disadvantage in respect to the increase of their numbers. They have to face the fact that they, like all the other celibate Communities, are rapidly declining. Every year sees their numbers diminished. Some of their villages have a half-deserted aspect. In nearly every one of their Societies there is a great preponderance of aged people. Of the thousands of children they have adopted few have remained among them after they reached maturity. "Since I came to this place, forty-nine years ago," said an Elder at North Union, "we have taken in young people enough to make a continuous line half a mile long; and I alone remain." "Out of eighty boys that went to school, in the course of five winters, with myself," says a recent seceder from the Hancock Society, "not one besides myself remained till he was twenty years old." The Shakers themselves are as well aware of their present lack of prosperity as their outside friends and critics; but they stand true to their principles and calling, and leave the rest to God. And if the homes they have made are not strong enough to hold their young people at the age when the world and the flesh offer the strongest inducements, they are yet warm enough with love and friendship and the presence of the Good Spirit to induce many wanderers from their circle to return, to find the contentment and rest they have sought elsewhere in vain. The story of many an humble Shaker would be full of instruction could it be written. I recall one that seemed to me to be of thrilling interest as I listened to its recital. Taken among the Shakers by his parents when a small boy, our hero had run away after some years—gone on to the lakes—gone into the far west and south—attached himself to a United States surveying and exploring party—married—lived among the Chippewas and other Indian tribes for years, until he learned their language and ways of life—until a life of roving and hunting, with its perils and excitements, its songs and camp-fires, was far more attractive to him than civilized life with all its artificial accessories—returning after twenty years to the home of self-denial and peace he had fled from in his youth, satisfied that it is the best place on earth for those 'who prefer the joys of the spirit to the vexations of the flesh. Singularly enough, his father, whose grave he pointed out among the evergreens, had had a similar experience—running away when a young man and the flesh was strong, and returning to mature in spirit for the hereafter. There is indeed, said my Shaker friend,

> "A divinity that shapes our ends,
> Rough-hew them how we will."

The Shakers have had thousands of secessions, and

many difficulties with seceders. These have from time to time been carried into the courts; and, as in the case of the Harmonists and Separatists, the result of trials at law has been to establish the following points, as epitomized by Judge Towner:

"1st. That Community contracts are not against public policy, nor contrary to any principle of law or morals.

"2d. That they are not in derogation of the inalienable right of liberty of conscience, but are really an exercise of that right.

"3d. That they are supported by a good and sufficient consideration, viz., one's support, etc., from the common fund while a member.

"4th. That they are maintainable and should be supported on the principles of the law of trusts and charitable uses as administered by courts of chancery.

"5th. That in adopting community of property persons are but following the example of the Apostles and adopting a rule ordained by them. Though this point might be claimed to be an *obiter dictum*, it is sustained by judges of the standing and fame of Justice McLean of the Supreme Court of the United States and Chief Justice Gibson of the Supreme Court of Pennsylvania.

"6th. That if such contract were illegal and void, a party to it could have no recovery against others, on the principle that they are in *pari delicto*, and the law leaves them where it finds them."

In Ohio the Society at Union Village had a great lawsuit long ago which settled the question whether persons can bequeath their property to a Community. Malcham Worley had left his property to that Society. His relatives set up the plea of insanity. The celebrated Tom Corwin appeared as counsel for the Shakers. "George Fox," he said, "wore leather breeches and did many eccentric things; Martin Luther threw his inkstand at the devil; but the Quakers will not admit that George Fox was crazy, and Protestants will not admit than Martin Luther was crazy; neither can it be allowed that Malcham Worley was crazy, because by a deed drawn by himself he chose to give his property to this peculiar people!"

The Shaker Families are examples of complete Communism, so far as the principle of celibacy permits. There is in them no combination of familism and Communism as in most of the Societies described in this work. And in their household industries, as well as in their principal businesses, they take great advantage of the principle of combination. Their bakeries, laundries, dairies, etc., are often models in this respect. The Communism of the Shakers does not, however, extend to different Families, except at Pleasant Hill, where the three central Families own their property together. One would suppose that at least the property of one Society, whether composed of one or ten Families, would be considered the common property of that Society. The Shakers themselves will say the property is more easily managed thus divided, and that in case of great loss by one Family the others help bear the burden. Thus I was told that a single Family contributed $3,000 toward the new dwelling of the Church Family at New Lebanon; and I have understood that the expense of publishing the organ of the Shakers is shared by all the Societies. But their divided interest results in inequalities, some Families and Societies having much more wealth than others.

The worship of the Shakers has always attracted much attention, and deservedly so. I attended several Shaker meetings at different places, and always with pleasure and profit.

The following sketch was written after a visit to the Canterbury Society in New Hampshire:

SHAKER WORSHIP.

How Conducted—Speeches—Songs and Marches—the Religious Element in Communities.

Shaker Village, N. H., June 12, 1876.

I AM not a Shaker, believing there is a better way, and am quite ready to see the Shakers' faults, as will duly appear; but for all that I will speak of the good I find. It has taken a century to live down the lies that have been told about them, and a good omen for Socialism is it that they are likely to have fairer play the next hundred years. Howells' article in the June *Atlantic* gives them a good send-off. It by no means tells the entire truth; but it does proclaim to a vast audience that this people, once so despised, persecuted and belied, are worthy examples in many respects to the whole Christian world.

Howells' account of their worship is indeed the most satisfactory of any that I have read. It makes the reader feel in a degree how sincere and earnest these consecrated people are. I say in a degree; for it is impossible for one not in spiritual accord with them to fully depict in words the meetings of the Shakers.

The Shakers have gatherings of some sort nearly every evening. Three evenings in the week are generally set apart for "union meetings." For these the brethren and sisters, from ten to twenty in number, as the case may be, come together either in the brothers' rooms or in rooms especially provided for the purpose, forming two ranks, the sexes sitting opposite each other; and spend an hour in conversation, or reading, or singing, as they choose. Only the Sunday meetings, in which all the Families of a Society take part, are open to the public; and that part of the public living

within ten miles of this village fully appreciates its privileges
in this respect. At the meeting here yesterday there were at
least two hundred strangers and visitors present. I am informed that during the summer months this number is sometimes doubled, compelling most of the Shaker brothers and sisters to absent themselves; and that those who are present are
often crowded into such close quarters that their "goings
forth in the dance" are necessarily omitted. The meetings here are indeed wonderfully attractive. Thirty-seven
carriages came yesterday from the towns near and distant, and
many people on foot. Probably the greater number attend
the meetings from mere curiosity; but some doubtless find
in them spiritual nutriment.

Yesterday there were present about thirty Shaker brothers
and fifty sisters. The exercises were begun by the reading of
an original anthem by one of the sisters, in a voice so clear
and distinct that every syllable was easily heard by the whole
assembly:

> "I looked, and lo! a multitude
> Stood on Mount Zion."

In the singing of this anthem and of the many hymns
which followed, I noticed that most of the worshipers took
part, including nearly every one of the sisters.

The anthem ended, a brother stepped into the space
separating the brothers and sisters—who in their worship are
always formed in ranks on opposite sides of the room, headed
respectively by the first elder and eldress—and in a few
appropriate words, adressed to both the believers and un-
believers present, indicated the object of the meeting and the
spirit in which it should be conducted, and expressed his
confidence that they should receive strength from on high.
Then about a dozen of the singers, brothers and sisters,
formed a parallelogram in the center of the room, and sang

> "O, tell me not of earthly wealth or favor,"

while all the others marched around them, singing and keeping time with hands and feet—their hands making a motion as if gathering something.

Then followed,

"Trust in me; trust in me,"

and

"The bright morning of the new creation;"

the singing growing more and more lively, and the marching approaching nearer and nearer to the dance, which it never quite reached.

The marching ceased. A brother, without leaving his position in the ranks, said:

"We have been singing, brothers and sisters, about a new relation. It occurs to me that I appreciate any thing new when it is better than the old; and the gospel relation is certainly better than the old relations of a selfish character. I rejoice that I can claim that relation with every one that is really at work for God's kindgom as his chief aim and object. I love to be in such good company; and I give you my pledge, brothers and sisters, that I will from this day strive to overcome all sin and wickedness and make my heart pure."

Such simple, earnest utterances as this were certain to draw forth short responses of approval or indorsement.

Then they sang, while all knelt down—

"Sweet angels, come nearer;
O, nearer and nearer.
Do list to our pleadings
For strength from on high.
This world's seeming pleasures,
Its riches, its honors,
The immortal spirit
Can never supply."

Then arising, a sister said she felt it was good to be there; that good angels would come nearer; that we have the promise if we draw near to God he will draw near to us; that divine power would be given us if we take up our cross against the sins of the world. She thanked God that she was not a slave in any sense of the word; that she possessed all her faculties, and could devote them to God and the virgin life. She was not ashamed of her calling; she rejoiced that she was called to separate herself from the world. Christians were to be the salt of the earth—she did not want to be without the savor.

Another was thankful that the Shakers had been called out of the generative order into a new and more excellent way of living—a virgin life; that their lives and conduct might be conformed to the angelic state.

Then marching was resumed, and became more and more exhilarating, while the really beautiful hymn was sung:

> "I've enlisted once forever,
>   In the cause of truth to stand;
> Beyond all doubts and fears
>   I give my heart and hand.
>
> "My feet have found the way,
>   My soul has heard the call;
> O heaven, give me strength
>   To triumph over all.
>
> "I fear the threat'ning storms
>   That may my sky o'ercast;
> The power of God alone
>   Will shield me from the blast.
>
> "What though my sun be hidden,
>   My faith I'll keep in view,
> The way of life I've chosen
>   With purpose firm and true."

This was followed by a slow march to the song,

> "Come ye out! come ye out!"

which reminded one how necessary it is to keep step, to follow the lead, as we march on toward heaven and life eternal: each should make his life an example that others may safely follow.

Then came the most effective discourse of the day by a sister—of whom Frederica Bremer wrote many years ago:

"She is of singular beauty, and a more fascinating, inspired glance than hers I never beheld." Hers is an inspirational nature; through her are given many of the songs which enter so largely into the worship and daily life of the Shakers. Here is one:

> "Ever changing, ever aiming
> Toward a higher, better life;
> Ever learning, ever earning,
> Is the good believer's strife.

> "Light unfolding, spirit molding,
> Is the law of endless growth;
> Feeding thought and word and action
> From the wells of boundless truth."

The burden of her utterance was *genuineness* in one's religious character. This seemed to her essential and above every other consideration. Form and ceremony are as the passing wind. To think of relying upon them would be only an irritation to her spirit. She consecrated her life anew. Her past life of self-denial had been glorious, and sufficient to lead her to continued consecration. She loved to recognize that the distance between her soul and its Maker was being spanned. Words had not power to express the love of God in her soul. She loved the virgin life; she loved her Savior, who bore the cross, and who is our example. Her work was individual—she must experience the work of God in her own soul. That is worth more than the whole world. But that work must be genuine. "The world loveth its own; it can never take us in. It is bound to maintain the generative life. We have the work of regeneration to maintain, as did our Savior. I love our cross. I will keep the purity of my heart toward all mankind. I will keep the solemn vow I make this morning."

Her discourse finished, there were more songs, more marching, more simple heart-utterances from the faithful brothers and sisters. Of the songs I was particularly impressed with the following, which appears to be a favorite in several of the Societies:

> "Number me with the Pilgrim band
> Who are traveling to the promised land,
> Giving to God both heart and hand,
> United for the truth to stand.

> "'Tis an uphill work we're called unto,
> An uphill march till we've traveled through;
> Then falter not, beloved few,
> For your reward is just and true."

They sang this with much spirit, marching the while with joyous step, and their countenances aglow with the fervor which can only come from a faith within.

There was great freedom—no hesitation—no awkward pauses—no useless formalities—no waiting for one another —the young and old alike were free. The earnest utterance of a young sister introducing a little song—

> "I would rather be a pure, white spirit"—

which others joined her in singing, should have touched many a heart. The sisters were indeed rather more prominent in the exercises than the brothers. This might be explained perhaps by the fact that some of the principal male speakers were absent holding a meeting in a distant village, in response to urgent and repeated solicitations; but the Shakers make no useless and unjust distinctions of sex, and are in this respect an example to most other denominations.

My sketch of Shaker worship is somewhat extended; but I am certain that it is impossible to understand the Shakers without comprehending pretty fully their religious ordinances, and especially their meetings. People inquire, "What holds the Shakers together?" I believe their meetings should have the principal credit. They are not all equally interesting—some that I have attended have been comparatively dull; but they all have this peculiarity, that every member who is present takes some part in the exercises—if not in speaking, then in singing or marching; and all must feel in some degree their harmonizing, unifying power. Mere doctrines, however good, will not hold people together for a century; it requires an afflatus; and this is dependent for its effects upon the assembling of the members together. And in this respect the Shakers are nearly as far from limiting themselves to a Sunday meeting as the Oneida Communists. Nearly every evening in the week witnesses some gathering for conversation, singing or worship. Perhaps Community builders will some day find a way to produce the requisite harmony and unity without appealing so strongly and persistently to the religious element; but facts thus far in the history of the world say nay.   W. A. H.

With this letter I close my account of the Shakers. Those interested will procure their paper and their books; while others will declare the Shaker life intolerable to a liberty-loving soul, and conclude that sufficient has been said of this singular people, who can truly boast that "for nearly a hundred years they have lived prosperous, contented, happy, making their land bloom like the fairest garden; and during all these years they have never spent a penny for police, for lawyers, for judges, for poor-houses, for penal institutions, or any like 'improvements' of the outside world." Should they cease to exist as organized bodies, their example would live and proclaim through all the ages the practicability of Communal Society based on Christian Brotherhood.

ONEIDA.

THESE Societies, like most of the Communities which have held together for any considerable period, laid first a religious foundation. Their builder, JOHN HUMPHREY NOYES, was called a "Perfectionist" as early as 1834, on account of the new doctrine he proclaimed, while yet a student in the Yale Theological Seminary, that the gospel of Christ ensures present salvation from sin. This was at least twelve years before he experimented in Communism. His doctrine of perfection had its complement in another doctrine equally at variance with the accepted dogmas of the popular churches of that day, namely, that Christ's Second Coming and the establishment of his eternal kingdom took place within a single generation from the time of his first coming. These views made Mr. Noyes an independent religionist, and in process of time, with the aid of the press and oral presentation, gave him a small following of disciples, in the Eastern and Middle States, who were known as "Perfectionists," or "Believers" as they more frequently called themselves. These constituted the material out of which was formed, first a small communal organization in Putney, Vermont, and in 1848 the Oneida Community, in Lenox, Madison Co., New York.

It is common to ascribe the success which has attended this Community solely to the great abilities of its founder; but Mr. Noyes himself has enumerated a number of "coöperating causes," among which he has placed first "the faithful help of a large body of men and women, whose moral power and business ability, if they had chosen other channels, would have made them individually successful in all the ordinary professions." These helpers include, in addition to several members of his father's family, many persons of high moral and social standing. Nordhoff's remark that "all the successful Communities are composed of what are called 'common people,'" is not strictly true, if by that remark is meant the laboring in distinction from the educated classes. The latter are well represented in the Oneida Community. Mr. Noyes studied at Amherst, Dartmouth, Andover and Yale; his father was a college graduate and tutor, a State Representative and Member of Congress; and the Noyeses are connected by blood and marriage with many who have won distinction in art, literature and politics. The Community includes two families of physicians, two men who have received a medical diploma since they became members of the O. C., four who have been educated as lawyers, several clergymen and families of clergymen, a number of graduates of Colleges and Scientific Schools, several editors and writers for the press; and, besides, the original members of the Community had generally a high standing in the churches and in society before they became Perfectionists or Communists, and they were all earnest, God-fearing men and women, who engaged in Communism because they felt called to the work. It is claimed, in short, that the members of the O. C. form "an average slice of humanity," and include, with the common laborers and mechanics, and those even who have suffered need, a fair proportion of the refined and cultured.

The buildings of the Community consisted at first of two small frame dwellings, a log-hut, and an old saw-mill, once owned by the Indians. It was a dozen years before their members got beyond the necessity of sleeping in garrets and out-houses. Though the means brought in by the members enabled them to live tolerably well at first, they soon learned to content themselves with the humblest fare. For years bread and milk, potatoes and beans, with milk gravy in lieu of butter, were the chief articles of diet. Their first meetings were held at the old log house: in the absence of chairs, persons sat on stairs, trunks, cradles, or whatever else they could find. Their Sunday gatherings, which at that time attracted outside people, were first held in an old barn; and after the "Mansion House," as they called it, was completed, their meeting- and dining-rooms were furnished with pine benches.

The industries of the Community were also at first of the simplest and rudest kinds: farming, logging, milling, and clearing swamps, in which latter occupation the women courageously engaged, as they did also in lathing and other work connected with the building of the first houses. There were no distinctions of classes in respect to labor, Mr. Noyes, the founder, taking the lead as mason in laying up chimneys and foundation-walls.

The Community treasury was frequently empty in those early days; it was not always easy to pay their postage; and they often could not tell a day beforehand where the money was coming from to buy the necessary groceries. Molasses was brought from the village store in a jug, and the sugar in a pail! Nothing but the strictest economy and adherence to the rule, "Pay as you go!" and above all the blessing of God, as they believe, kept them from the financial ruin which continually threatened. As it was, during the first nine years of pioneer work the Community reduced its capital from $107,000 to $67,000; but in the same time it improved its organization, developed important principles and measures, and started several businesses, some of which have

proved fairly remunerative. The Community has since
prospered financially until its property (including that of
the W. C. branch) is now estimated at a little more than half
a million dollars—not a large sum considering the number of
its members, and a small one compared with what has been
accumulated by some other Communities.

These Communists with their radical institutions naturally
excited prejudice at first among their neighbors and the surrounding population, who had no knowledge of the peaceable
character and intentions of the people who had settled in their
midst. The Communists themselves were perhaps less prudent than they have since become, and there were collisions
of one kind and another with outsiders which led to legal
complications; and at one time they actually contemplated a
dissolution. But the best men of the vicinity said, "No; you
have proved yourselves peaceable and industrious citizens;
and we are unwilling you should leave." Thus the tide was
turned, the danger passed, and the Community has from that
time steadily grown in the favor of good people far and near.

The Oneida Community attracts more visitors than any
other of the American Communities — perhaps more than
all others. They come from Maine and California, from
England and France and other foreign countries; while ex-
cursion parties from the surrounding cities and villages are
common during the summer months. These are occasionally
more than a thousand strong. Indeed, as many as fifteen
hundred persons have visited the Community grounds in a
single day. Visitors receive polite attention, and all respectful
questions pertaining to their principles and practical life are
frankly answered. Inquiring visitors often propound such
questions and receive such replies as those which follow:

"What is the present number of the Oneida Community
including its Wallingford branch?"

"There are here at O. C. 268; at Wallingford 38: in all 306."

"How are the sexes divided?"

"There are 145 males and 161 females."

"How many children are there?"

"60 under 14 years of age; 82 under 21."

"What nationalities are represented in the Community?"

"We have a few English; the rest are Americans."

"Do you practice temperance?"

"We use neither tobacco nor alcoholic liquors."

"Do you use tea and coffee?"

"Both are discarded. Decoctions of roasted grain, etc., with cocoa, take their place."

"Are you vegetarians?"

"No; but we use less meat than most people and more fruit."

"Do you use unbolted wheat?"

"Not exclusively, but it is much in favor."

"How do you manage to suit so many in regard to kinds of food and times of eating?"

"Meals are served at 10 A. M. and 4 P. M., with a lunch at 6 in the morning, for the children and such as prefer a hygienic table; at 7 A. M. and 1 P. M., with a lunch at 6 P. M., for those who prefer a less restricted diet."

"How are your women employed?"

"They do the housework with the assistance of a few of the men and half a dozen hired people in the kitchen; they work in the sewing-room, in the printing-office and counting-room, in the children's department and in the school-room, etc."

"Do you believe in the equality of men and women?"

"No; we don't believe even in the equality of men: but we do believe that every man, woman and child should be surrounded with circumstances favoring the best development of heart, mind and body, and that no one should be excluded on account of age, sex, or race, from engaging in any occupation for which he or she is adapted by nature or culture."

"Do Community women talk much about their rights?"

"No; there is no occasion for that: they have all the rights they desire. One of them thus defines the position of woman in the Community:

"'Communism gives woman, without a claim from her, the place which every true woman most desires, as the free and honored companion of man. Communism emancipates her from the slavery and corroding cares of a mere wife and mother; stimulates her to seek the improvement of mind and heart that will make her worthy a higher place than ordinary society can give her. Freed from forced maternity, a true and holy desire for children grows in her heart. Here no woman's hand is red with the blood of innocents, as is whispered so often of many of her sisters in bondage. Gradually, as by natural growth, the Community women have risen to a position where, in labor, in mind, and in heart, they have all and more than all that is claimed by the women who are so loudly asserting their rights. And through it all they have not ceased to love and honor the truth that 'the man is the head of the woman,' and that woman's highest, God-given right is to be 'the glory of man.'"

"You remarked that there were about half a dozen hired assistants in the kitchen; how many outsiders do you employ in all your departments of industry?"

"From one hundred to two hundred and fifty, according to the necessities of our businesses."

"How do you reconcile the hireling system with Communism?"

"We do not reconcile them. We expect that Communism will sometime become general and that hiring will cease; in the meantime we propose to help our neighbors and ourselves by furnishing remunerative labor to those who are not prepared for Communism. Many of our workmen, besides supporting themselves and families, have laid by a part of their wages, and some have been able to build houses, while a few have bought small farms."

"How are your men employed?"

"They work in all our departments; in some of them doing most of the manual labor; in others being mainly employed as superintendents."

"Don't some of your people, who have had the superintendence of outside workers, come to feel above manual labor?"

"If there is a tendency of that kind it is likely to be corrected by the frequent changes made in our superintendents, by our system of criticism, and by the public opinion of the Community, which considers all kinds of labor alike honorable."

"Are superintendents of the different departments elected or appointed?"

"Both; *i. e.*, the leaders exercise at their option the appointing power, generally with pretty free consultation with others; and the Business Board at its option elects persons to fill particular posts of responsibility, subject to the approval of the leaders."

"Who compose the Business Board?"

"The heads of departments and all who choose to attend its sessions, both male and female."

"Don't the Business Board and the leaders of the Community sometimes differ in their judgments?"

"We don't recall any serious case of that kind. We seek harmony and work for unanimity, and defer the execution of any plan so long as it meets with decided opposition from even a small minority."

"What has been the influence of the Community upon surrounding population?"

"Ask our neighbors. We think they will testify that it has from the first favored education, good habits, sound morality. They are glad to work for us, and to have their children employed in our factories. Then it is certain that wherever the Communists have settled there has been a great rise in the value of real estate."

"Is the Community managed by one man?"

"No; there are at least as many managers as there are departments of business. The larger businesses, as the Trap, Silk and Fruit-Packing, are under the supervision of Boards or Committees, organized by, or with the approval of, the General Business Board of the Community. Besides, all questions of considerable importance are brought before the Community for decision, and in the general assembly every person, male and female, has a voice and vote."

"But don't some have much more influence than others?"

"Of course: that is true of every organization. The best and wisest ought to rule every-where."

"Are persons allowed to leave the Community?"

"Certainly."

"Can they take away any property?"

"Our practice has been to refund to seceders all the property they brought into the Community, or its equivalent in money, and to give those who had no property when they joined a good outfit of clothing and one hundred dollars, in case of their peaceable withdrawal. But our present Covenant cuts off all claim on the part of seceders, and leaves the matter of refunding any property entirely at the option of the Community."

"Why was this change made?"

"To test more thoroughly the sincerity of applicants for admission, and to avoid trouble in cases of secession."

"Have you any formulated creed?"

"No."

"But you have religious doctrines which are generally accepted by the members of the Community?"

"Yes; our people generally believe in the Bible as 'the text-book of the Spirit of Truth,' and as a record of 'supernatural facts and sensible communications from God;' that God is a dual being—Father and Son; that 'evil comes from the Devil as good comes from God;' that God was in no sense the author of evil; that a 'dispensation of grace commenced at the manifestation of Christ entirely different from the preceding dispensation;' that salvation from sin is 'the special promise and gift of the new dispensation,' and is apprehended by faith in the resurrection of Christ; that Christ came the second time and established his everlasting kingdom, according to promise, within one generation of his first coming; that we are now living in 'the dispensation of the fullness of times,' and that the final judgment is approaching; that 'the divine obligation to specially observe one day of the week passed away with the first or Jewish dispensation,' as also many other external observances; that the baptism of the Holy Spirit is the only baptism recognized in the new dispensation; that personal communication with Christ is a privilege of the Gospel, and when this communication is perfected it will ensure salvation from all evil, including disease and death, etc. etc. But the doctrine regarded as most essential to Communism is that of salvation from sin through Christ."

"Will you explain more fully the meaning and scope of this doctrine?"

"Mr. Noyes has said: 'Salvation from sin, as we understand it, is not a system of duty-doing under a code of dry laws, Scriptural or natural; but is a special phase of religious experience, having for its basis spiritual intercourse with God. All religionists of the positive sort believe in a personal God, and assume that he is a sociable being. This faith leads them to seek intercourse with him, to approach him by prayer, to give him their hearts, to live in communion with him. These exercises, and the various states and changes of the inner life connected with them, constitute the staple of what is called religious experience. We cannot live in familiar intercourse with human beings without becoming better or worse under their influence; and certainly fellowship with God must affect still more powerfully all the springs of action. We hold that intercourse with God may proceed so far as to destroy selfishness in the heart, and so make an end of sin. In other words, our Communism with one another is based on our religion, and our religion is based on Communism with God and the good spirits of the invisible world.' "

"What attitude do you take in regard to the developments of modern Spiritualism?"

" We have investigated the various phenomena with some care and patience. Some of our own members have been found to possess considerable mediumistic powers, enabling them to procure rappings, table-tippings, writing, etc.; and those among us who have been more directly interested in the subject have had sittings with the most celebrated mediums of this country. Our experience thus far leads us to believe that many of the manifestations are genuine; *i. e.*, that they are the acts of unseen intelligences purporting to be the spirits of the dead. But at present these genuine manifestations are so mixed up with trickery and deception that investigations must be made with great caution to avoid being misled. Although we are much interested in the subject, and think it has an important bearing on our future, yet we use great deliberation in drawing conclusions, and do not reverence the spirits which communicate through the mediums as being our superiors in any important sense. On the contrary, we take the liberty to criticise them and their influence freely, which we have come to think is the only safe way to deal with them."

" What are the social principles of the Community ? "

" We recognize no claim of individual property in one another. We affirm that the same spirit which on the day of Pentecost abolished exclusiveness in regard to money tends to obliterate all other property distinctions. But we have no affiliation with those commonly termed Free Lovers, because their principles and practices seem to us to tend toward anarchy. Our Communities are *families*, as distinctly bounded and separated from promiscuous society as ordinary households. The tie that binds us together is as permanent and sacred, to say the least, as that of common marriage, for it is our religion. We receive no new members (except by deception and mistake) who do not give heart and hand to the family interest for life and forever. Community of property extends just as far as freedom of love. Every man's care and every dollar of the common property are pledged for the maintenance and protection of the women and the education of the children of the Community."

" Your people and the Shakers appear to be directly opposed in principle. Is there any friendly intercourse between the two Societies ? "

" O, yes."

" How is that possible ? They consider generation all wrong, and you think persons can propagate without being degraded or sensualized by it."

" Do you state the position of the Shakers correctly ? As we understand them, they do not object to the increase of the race *per se*, but only insist that it belongs to the natural order and not to the spiritual. We sympathize most sincerely with their purpose to lead pure and sinless lives, and are even ready to admit that Ann Lee might have acted under a wise afflatus in calling her followers away from everything connected with propagation. With only two alternatives, celibacy or propagation unrestricted and unmodified by science, what strong reasons there are in favor of choosing the first alternative! But a century has passed since the founder of Shakerism lived—a century replete with discoveries of new truth bearing upon the subject of human generation. The great principles lying at the foundation of stirpiculture, or the scientific propagation of human beings, have been evolved; and it is conceivable that were Ann Lee now living she might call on her followers to leave their stronghold of celibacy, and advance into this broad field, carrying with them the self-control, self-denial, self-purification that a century's battle with the lusts of the flesh has given them! We cannot say that we have reason to anticipate any such progress on their part, and hence there is likely to be in the future, as there has been in the past, a wide difference between the two Societies on this important subject. They think there can be no Christian Communism or Christian life without celibacy. We think the time has arrived for something better, and that all the good they find in celibacy with all the benefits that result from the association of the sexes may be realized in Christian Communism. And certainly if Communism is to flourish in this world on any great scale, or even perpetuate itself, it must progress beyond the celibate condition. But we have great respect for the Shakers, and honor them for their labors and successes."

"Are the children of the Community healthy and happy?"

"Our own testimony on this point might savor of partiality, and so I will read to you what Goldwin Smith published in the *Canadian Monthly* after a visit to the Community. He certainly will not be suspected of a wish to represent any feature of Communism too favorably; but he says—

"'The children are regarded as children of the Community, and are brought up together on that footing. The mother is allowed to take part in nursing them as much as she pleases, but she is not required to do more. Undeniably they are a fine, healthy-looking, merry set of infants.....The Oneida children are reared under conditions of exceptional advantage, which could not fail to secure health to the offspring of any but positively diseased parents....The nurseries with every thing about them are beautiful. Large play-rooms are provided for exercise in winter. The nurses are not hirelings, but members of the Community who voluntarily undertake the office. Every precaution is taken against the danger of infection. A simple and wholesome dietary is enforced, and no mother or grandmother is permitted to ruin digestion and temper, by administering first a poison from the confectioner's and then another poison from the druggist's.'"

"Will you explain more fully the arrangements of your Children's House? How much care, for instance, does the mother have of her child?"

"She has the *exclusive* care of her child until the time of weaning, which in most cases takes place at nine months, though about this there is no rule except the one of common sense. Care is taken as to the time of year, the state of the child in regard to teething and other conditions. When well weaned the child enters the first department of the Children's House, where there are others of nearly the same age who are cared for by nurses, who serve half a day at a time. The child leaves its mother at 8 o'clock in the morning, and returns to her again at 5 o'clock in the afternoon, remaining with her through the night. At about a year and a half, according to the degree of development, the child passes into the second department, where it remains all day. The par-

ents are free at any time to take the child away for a walk or
a ride or a visit at their room.　While it is in this department
the mother, however, gradually gives up all particular responsibility about its clothing, diet and night-care.　She is then
free to fill her place in the various industries of the household.　There is still a third department, which the child enters
at about three years, and in which it continues until the age
of thirteen or fourteen, when it leaves the department altogether.　Through this entire period, as in the previous ones,
no mother is separated from her child for any considerable
time.　We aim to deal with our children according to the dic-
tates of the most enlightened common sense combined with
a tender regard for human weakness ; but how to bring them
up under the best moral, spiritual, intellectual, physical and
social conditions has been a problem requiring the deepest
study on the part of the Community for many years.　If the
parents were to keep the exclusive or even the principal care
of their children, Communism would be difficult, and there
would be, besides, great waste of force.　We have found that
the more fully different functions, like that of child-training,
can be differentiated, the more economical will be the workings of the institution ; and it is imperative that economies
of this kind be studied, or a Community would be a great
lumbering machine, increasing instead of saving labor.　By
such differentiation, and by placing in special charge of the
children, after they are weaned, the persons who are best
fitted for the responsibility, while parents are left at liberty to
associate with their children freely, so far as such association
does not militate with the best interests of either, we claim
to have made considerable improvement upon the common
way of rearing children."

"Very likely ; but I can see that the system might occasionally result in trials to parents; and now let me ask

whether your form of life does not have, along with its many comforts, many things hard to be borne?"

"Certainly, it has. Our Society is based on the idea that selfishness must be displaced in all the relations of life; and that is a work which cannot be accomplished without suffering of the keenest kind. But to the earnest lover of improvement it brings its present rewards; and then we comfort ourselves with the assurance that whatever makes us harmonic and altruistic here will help us in 'the beyond.'"

"Has the Community any literature of its own?"

"The Press has been almost constantly employed by Mr. Noyes and his followers since 1834. The first handbills and tracts were followed by a monthly paper, *The Perfectionist;* this by *The Witness*, issued irregularly; this by *The Perfectionist* again; then came *The Spiritual Magazine;* then the *Free Church Circular;* then twelve volumes of the first series of *The Circular*, including one semi-weekly and one tri-weekly volume; then the second series, the eighth volume of which was commenced Jan. 1, 1871, with its name changed to *Oneida Circular*. Pamphlets and books have been printed from time to time, including *The Way of Holiness*, the *Berean*, three *Annual Reports of the Oneida Community*, the *Religious Experience of J. H. Noyes*, *Bible Communism*, *Faith Facts*, the *Trapper's Guide*, *Hand-Books of the Oneida Community*, *Male Continence*, *Scientific Propagation*, *Mutual Criticism*, *History of American Socialisms*, *Foot-Notes by Alfred Barron*, *Home-Talks by J. H. Noyes*, etc., etc. Many of these works are now out of print."

"What is the secret of your unity?"

"More than thirty years ago a few persons recognized Mr. J. H. Noyes as an embodiment of a higher Christian life, and acknowledged him as their leader. The unity then begun has never been broken nor its power of cohesion weakened, but has

increased with the increase of members and the wear and
tear of experience. Goldwin Smith speaks of Mr. Noyes as
'a man whose ability is written on his brow, on the pages of
his vigorously written books, and on the work of his organizing hands;' but we recognize in him something more than

JOHN HUMPHREY NOYES.

natural 'ability.' To us he is a permanent medium of the
spirit of Christ."

"What are the conditions of membership?"

"We insist that candidates shall, first, understand and
hold by heart our religious and social doctrines; secondly,

count the cost of enlisting with us for life; thirdly, secure their freedom from any claims of kindred, etc., that might entangle us; and, fourthly, pay all their debts. Joining the Community is like marriage; and these are simply the prudent preliminaries of such a decisive act. If the parties are not in full sympathy, or are in external circumstances unfavorable to a union, it is better for them to remain friends than to venture on a closer connection."

The Community has a library of between five and six thousand volumes, and keeps the best magazines and journals on file, accessible to all the members.

There is a school-building; and it is the purpose of the Community to give all its children good educational advantages.

A play-house has been erected for the children at a cost of $1,000, within convenient distance of the home buildings. Amusements in the Community are subject only to such restrictions as are required by good order.

There is a photographic studio, and attention to the fine arts is encouraged.

The Community has a summer-resort at Oneida Lake, twelve miles distant, which is frequented by parties for fishing, hunting and general recreation.

The Community has 580 acres of good land, which is devoted to meadow and pasturage, orchards and vineyards, and the raising of vegetables and fruits for their canning or preserving establishment; for which they harvested in 1877 six acres of beans, eight acres of raspberries, 5,000 bushels of tomatoes, 5,224 bushels of sweet corn, and other crops in more limited quantities.

Their dairy is pronounced one of the best in the country, and includes 50 Ayrshires, 7 Holsteins, 56 grades and natives. They have 45 horses and colts.

Shoemaking, tailoring, dentistry, printing, carpentry, and other common trades, are carried on; but the capital and industry of the Community are mainly concentrated in three businesses: canning of fruits and vegetables, and the manufacture of silk and of steel traps.

The present dwellings of the Community are of brick. The principal one is 188 feet by 70, with a rear extension of 100 feet. A new dwelling is in process of construction, which with its wings will have a south front of 112 feet, a west front of 103 feet, and a north front of 149 feet. The principal part will be four stories high, and will have a one-story connection, 30 by 42 feet, with the main dwelling, to be used as a library and reading-room in place of the present one.

The home buildings are heated by steam. Steam is also found an invaluable aid in their laundry and kitchen, where it is made to do much of the work. The greatest advantage is taken of machinery and labor-saving contrivances in both of these departments. The dining-rooms are located immediately above the kitchen in a building disconnected from the main dwellings.

For securing good order and the improvement of the members, the Community place much reliance upon a peculiar system of plain speaking, which they term *Mutual Criticism.* They have described this system in a pamphlet. Its origin is traced to a secret society of missionary brethren, with which Mr. Noyes was connected while preparing himself for missionary labor and pursuing theological studies at Andover Seminary. The members of this society submitted themselves in turn to the sincerest comment of one another as a means of personal improvement. Mr. Noyes observed and experienced its great benefits, and subsequently introduced it into the Oneida Community as a regular means of discipline. It is their principal agency of government. They have a standing committee of criticism, which is selected by the Community, and changed from time to time, thus giving all an opportunity to serve both as critics and subjects, and justifying the term "mutual" which they give to their criticism. The subject is made free to have others besides the committee present, or to have critics only of his own choice, or to invite an expression from the whole Community. The Communists say of the practical application of this system:

"It is not easy to overestimate the usefulness of criticism in its relation to Community life. There is hardly a phase of that life in which it does not play an important part. It is the regulator of industry and amusement—the incentive to all improvement—the corrector of all excesses. It governs and guides all. Criticism, in short, bears nearly the same relation to Communism which the system of judicature bears to ordinary society. As society cannot exist without government, and especially without a system of courts and police, so *Communism requires for its best development Free Criticism.*

"Our object being self-improvement, we have found by much experience that free criticism—faithful, honest, sharp truth-telling—is one of the best exercises for the attainment of that object. We have tried it thoroughly; and the entire body of the Community have both approved and honestly submitted themselves to it. Criticism is in fact the entrance-fee by which all the members have sought admission.

"In the great majority of cases criticism is desired and solicited by individuals, because they are certain from their own past experience, or from observation of the experience of others, that they will be benefited by it; but in some instances, where it is noticed that persons are suffering from faults or influences that might be corrected or removed by criticism, they are advised to submit themselves to it. In extreme cases of disobedience to the Community regulations, or obsession by influences adverse to the general harmony, criticism is administered by the Community or its leaders without solicitation on the part of the subject. In general, all are trained to criticise freely, and to be criticised without offense. Evil in character or conduct is thus sure to meet with effectual rebuke from individuals, from platoons, or from the whole Community.

"We only claim for our system of criticism that it is a new and improved application of old principles. Common society is not exempt from criticism. Thought is free, and faults draw censure wherever they exist. Every person is more or less transparent to those around him, and passes in the surrounding sphere of thought for pretty much what he is worth. Speech is free, too, in a certain way, and industriously supplies the demand for criticism with an article commonly called backbiting. If you have faults, you may be sure they are the measure of the evil-thinking and evil-speaking there is going on about you. Supply meets demand, but not in a way to tell to your account under the common system of distribution. Criticism is not more free with us, but it is distributed more profitably. We have a systematic plan of distribution, by which criticism is delivered in the right time and place, and in a way to produce the best results. Criticism as it goes in society is without method; there is no 'science' in it; it acts every-where like the electric fluid, but is not applied to any useful purpose; it distributes *itself*, and sometimes injuriously. In the Community we draw it off from the mischievous channels of evil-thinking and scandal, and apply it directly to the improvement of character."

The Community have another ordinance which they regard as of great importance to their harmony and general progress, *viz., Daily Evening Meetings.* These are of an hour's duration, and are conducted with very little formality. Matters of business, of Community order and government, the news of the day, scientific discussion, home lectures, religious testimony and discourse, music, and every thing of common interest, here come in for their share of attention. There is of course a moderator, but every member is free to take part in both the presentation and discussion of subjects. There are short-hand reporters, who note down for permanent record or transmission to the sister Community matters of special importance.

The Community have no definite regulations respecting hours of rising and of labor, leaving such matters for the most part to the judgment and inclination of the individual members; and they have little trouble from the lazy and shiftless. Where reproof or counsel is needed it is given through their system of criticism already described.

Several of the Communities have fallen upon similar customs respecting labor; one of which is to work *en masse*, or muster together in "bees" for the performance of certain definite enterprises. At Aurora-Bethel those who work in shops turn out when there is an urgent demand for labor in the harvest-field; and the same occurs at Zoar and Amana, men, women and children all working with common zeal for the common weal. At Economy, when the work of the harvest crowded, all hands used to join in the work, enlivening the labor with their German songs. Of the Harmonists it was written years ago: "Sometimes nearly the whole force of the Society, male and female, is put to one object, such as pulling flax, reaping, hoeing corn, etc., so that the labor of a hundred-acre field is accomplished in a day or two." The Oneidians have always made great account of this custom, as a means of increasing both the attractiveness and also the productiveness of labor. In earlier days they had "bees" for cutting and husking corn, working in the hay-field, harvesting peas, beans, etc., in which men and women and children took part with great enthusiasm. At present these occasions of gregarious industry are more confined to indoor labor, taking volunteers by scores to the kitchen, laundry and fruit-packing room ; but there are still occasional outdoor "bees," especially in the harvesting of fruit.

In common with the Shakers and Harmonists the Oneida Communists have some peculiarities of dress. They are, however, confined to the women, who wear a costume which originated in the Community, consisting of short dress and pantalets. They are enthusiastic in praise of its convenience. They exercise their individual taste respecting materials, colors, etc. The women have also adopted the practice of wearing short hair, which also saves time and vanity.

The Oneida Communists, like the Shakers, Harmonists and other Communists, are long-lived. Several have lived to be over four score years. They give much attention to hygienic conditions, living on simple food and following after temperance in all things. Among other health-maintaining and health-restoring agencies, their Turkish baths deserve mention. Then they have a theory that physical disease often roots back in spiritual disease, and that cleansing the spirit through criticism may sometimes restore the body to health. However this may be, the fact remains that their sick generally recover and live to ripe old age. Perhaps credit is due also to the facilities which such a Community has for taking care of the sick. A large Community naturally accumulates the conveniences which belong to a first-class hospital, and in addition has at command cheerful and experienced nurses such as few hospitals can supply.

Though the Community claim that their system is founded on religion and they have little faith in the success of any system of Communism which has not a religious basis, yet they are practical rather than theoretical religionists, and are

far enough from being formalists. Their reverence even for
the Bible is reverence for its spirit rather than its letter.
They pay little attention to the ordinances deemed so important by many sects. They are not afraid that religion will
suffer from any truth which science may discover; and the
works of Huxley and Tyndall, Darwin and Spencer, are well
represented in their library. Neither do they believe that
religion necessarily expresses itself in ascetic forms. Hence
their freedom to encourage education, art, music, amusements,
and every thing which tends to human culture or happiness,
only insisting that the element of self-seeking shall be excluded, and that the general Community interest shall be regarded
as paramount in every thing.

WALLINGFORD.

The Oneida Community has started at different times several small branch societies; but that at Wallingford, Connecticut, is the only one at present existing. It was founded in
1851, and now has a domain of 366 acres, including a small
lake that furnishes an excellent water-power. Its membership
has varied from twenty-five to eighty, according to the demands of its businesses. In addition to farming and horticul-
ture, it has carried on several branches of manufactures. It
had at one time a silk-factory; for several years a printing
establishment, which attracted work from the neighboring
villages and cities; at present the manufacture of spoons takes
the lead.

Perfect unity of interests exists between the Oneida and
Wallingford Communities. Men and means are freely ex-
changed as occasion requires. The property of the two Com-

munities is indeed the common property of the members of both. They also have the same principles, the same customs, the same means of discipline and of improvement. A journal of the important events happening at each Community is regularly transmitted to the other, and read publicly at the evening meeting, which is an institution of both.

A Community mansion was erected at Wallingford in the summer of 1876, but its buildings and accommodations are more limited than at Oneida, necessitating a smaller Community. Each place has, however, its peculiar attractions, and there are advantages in having the two Communities thus connected. Those who prefer a smaller family than that at Oneida, or a larger one than that at Wallingford, can be suited; and it is found agreeable to nearly all to occasionally change their residence from one to the other.

The Wallingford Community has a pleasant place on Long Island Sound, much visited during the summer months by parties from both Communities.

Should the Oneida Community establish other branch Societies they would only extend the unity that now exists between the two Communities of Oneida and Wallingford.

THE BROTHERHOOD OF THE NEW LIFE.

THIS is the name by which a considerable number of people in this and other countries, who have chosen THOMAS L. HARRIS as their leader, prefer to be known. They have attracted much attention, partly on account of the peculiarity of their principles, and partly because the Brotherhood has included persons of high social position and eminent talent, notably Lady Oliphant, widow of Sir Anthony Oliphant, C. B., formerly Chief-Justice of Ceylon; and Lawrence Oliphant, her son, who, after serving his government in diplomatic positions in China and Japan, gave up his seat in the English Parliament that he might take part in the social experiment of the Brotherhood at Salem-on-Erie, where their largest Family is located, called by the outside world the Brocton or Harris Community.

Previous to his connection with the Brotherhood Mr. Harris had made himself widely known, first as an eloquent Universalist preacher, then as a Spiritualist and the author of some of the best poems in Spiritualistic literature, and still later as one of the leaders of the Mountain-Cove Community in Virginia, a short-lived Spiritualistic Society.

Fourteen years intervened between the Mountain-Cove experiment in 1853 and the founding of Salem-on-Erie—years of trial and battle and growth, we may suppose, for Mr. Harris. During this period he became a leader of Christian Spiritualism against Infidel Spiritualism; spent several years in England preaching strange doctrines; lived five or six years at Amenia, Dutchess County, New York, where he prospered as a banker and agriculturist, and gathered about him a circle of devoted disciples.

The Brotherhood claim to have evoluted out of Communism; but as they at one time held their property in common, and still carry it on together, and possess many other communistic features both in theory and practice, and are, moreover, popularly regarded as Communists, I have thought it proper to give in the present work such information as I have been able to gather of their Societies; and, happily, it comes for the most part directly from Mr. Harris himself, who has most kindly responded to my inquiries. If, therefore, the account which follows is less sensational than some accounts that have been published, it will, nevertheless, have the interest which attaches to a true record:

THE BROTHERHOOD OF THE NEW LIFE AS DESCRIBED BY ITS LEADER.

Fountain Grove, Santa Rosa, Cal., Aug. 22, 1877.

W. A. HINDS, *Dear Sir:—*

The life, system and action of the Society which I represent are so far removed from the lines of the usual thought, that I fear I shall hardly be able to answer your friendly inquiries with the fullness you desire. Personally, I am not a Communist. I find it impossible to maintain the ordinary relations; much more to unite in close association, communistically, with even my nearest friends. My home is practically an hermitage: the evolution of my faculties has led me into strict natural celibacy. Whatever material property I possess is considered by me as fully my own; yet not my own, being held, like all other gifts, as a trust from God, for his service in the race. Both physically and morally I find it impossible to exist under other conditions.

While thus self-contained, reserved and isolated, I find myself enzoned by a large circle of men and women, in Europe and Asia, as well as in this country, who have been driven to me by a potent attraction, in the course of my labors, but without any conscious endeavor of my own. My life is devoted to their service, and I feel honored in their inexpressible love and devotion. They constitute the Society known as the "Brotherhood of the New Life." Of their numbers, wealth, or potential force, I do not feel at liberty to speak.

My people, with few exceptions, reside in isolated families, and esteem it fortunate that thus far they have generally escaped the intrusive curiosity of the civilizees. This is a kingdom that does not come with observation: it employs no verbal preachers: it practices no ecclesiastical rites: it seeks no mere natural proselytes: its voice is not heard in the street. Yet it affects no mystery, and those who desire to know of it for "the good of life" find no difficulty in attaining to what they seek. It grows simply by its power of organic diffusion and assimilation. We believe it to be a germ of the Kingdom of Heaven, dropped from upper space and implanted in the bosom of the earthly humanity:—in fine, the seed of a new order; the initial point for a loftier and sweeter evolution of man.

Two only of our Families, so far as I am aware, have fallen under the eye of correspondents of the press; that in the town of Portland, Chautauqua Co., N. Y., and this, my private residence, in California. These are practically one. In both of them the social order may perhaps be termed patriarchal, there being no community of possessions. I may quote from the old dramatist, and say: "A poor house, sir, but mine own." I hope I shall not trespass on the modest privacy of my guests and kinsmen, if I add that, under no stress of compulsion, but in the evolution of character, they have become, in the natural sense, celibate as I am: some entering from a state of monogamic marriage, but others virginal from the first.

Of the other Families in the Society, I may say that they are in different stages of advancement, from a starting-point of accepted altruism; that they begin from germs of individual households, with no break in the continuity of relations; the new growth forming in the old wood of the tree; the internal first changing, and then, by evolution, "that which is without" becoming "as that which is within." All growths are first invisible. After seventeen years of life, unity and struggle, the Brotherhood begins to declare its presence and purpose. Notices that you may have seen of it, like the sensational article in the *New York Sun*, published some years since, have been unauthorized accounts, and such facts as served to give them color and credence were obtained under the express understanding that they should be held in honorable confidence. In evolving a new spiritual experience, through a new social experience, we have sought to avoid publicity. It is time enough to describe a tree when it begins to ripen its fruit.

The Family at

SALEM-ON-ERIE,

which these press notices have brought into unwelcome observation, under the *pseudonym* of the "Brocton Community," was founded in the town of Amenia, Dutchess Co., N. Y., in the spring of 1861. It removed to its present locality in, I think, 1867. In Dr. Taylor's "History of Portland," which I mail to your address, you will find a brief *résumé* of its material and industrial affairs and of its labors at the date of publication, 1873. During the ensuing year the Family began to contract its affairs. Its industries are now confined to the orchard, vineyard and farm. Never so united, never so effective in unity, it maintains a waiting attitude.

This Family passed, years ago, through the communistic phase, in which, however, I did not take part, though esteeming it a phase in evolution and serving it financially. As a means of education it was useful, but those engaged in it found that, in the long run, it was neither promotive of their happiness, nor evolutionary in the direction of their ruling tendencies.

Without dissension or disunion, its members then passed into a phase of modified Socialism, each series constituting a family partnership, and found that this mode of combined action developed a large force of individual character, as well as a more strict business habit and aptitude. Here the ledger showed a favorable balance, but the spirit was not fully satisfied.

Meantime I organized my own affairs, amidst my friends, and employed all who did not fit or find place elsewhere, treating them as sons, but insisting on paying weekly wages. After a time they found it incompatible with their forming affections to receive money-pay.

I then entertained them as guests, brethren and children in their father's house; and this satisfied. They labor for me, and I for them: their services, recreations and expenses are regulated among themselves. I put limits on their labors, but not on their recreations or expenses. There is no espionage: honor rules: love is supreme. Gradually the family partnerships have ceased, without a struggle, and all have entered into this order.

In serving me these tender hearts believe that they are also serving God, working for a kingdom of universal righteousness. They do not think that I possess any thing, except as representatively; nor that I rule in them, except as aiding to lift and direct them into a larger freedom, wisdom and purity. I consider the Family at Salem-on-Erie and that at

Fountain Grove as one: the germ of a solar family in the midst of a planetary family system.

I find no difficulty in the solution of the painful and perplexing problem of the sexes. Monogamists who enter into union with me rise, by changes of life, into a desire for the death of natural sexuality. Those whose lives have been less strict first, perhaps, may pass through the monogamic relation, though not always; but the end is the same. Others, who have lived singly, holding the fierce passion in restraint, find themselves gliding out of the passional tempest into a bodily state of serenity and repose. Still I do not believe that sexlessness characterizes man in his higher and final evolution.

Among my people, as they enter into the peculiar evolution that constitutes the new life, two things decrease: the propagation of the species and physical death. In the large patriarchal Family that I have described but one death has occurred since its formation in 1861, and this under circumstances and with results which demonstrated to us that the dear and honored subject of the visitation was simply taken from his more visible place to serve as an intermediate for higher services. One young pair in our borders have had three children, I am sorry to say; but with this exception the births in seventeen years have been but two, and of these the younger is almost a young man. We think that generation must cease till the sons and daughters of God are prepared for the higher generation, by evolution into structural, bi-sexual completeness, above the plane of sin, of disease, or of natural mortality.

I have considered my Family, since 1861, merely as a school: its methods educationary, and its form only tentative. My aim, *per se*, has been neither to organize close nor far-apart association, but to prepare myself and the inmates of my house for *a new era of human evolution,* which we have considered to be at hand, and which in individual cases we think has now begun. We think that by the survival of the fittest, the most plastic, the most complex organisms, men of a new spirit wrought bodily into new structures, the race will take a new departure; that we approach a new beginning of human days and generations.

I may add here that our views are not the result of mere scriptural study, nor based on textual interpretations, and that we have no especial sympathy that unites us to one school of religionists more than to another. If we find one vein of knowledge, or possibly correct surmise, in Swedenborg, we find other veins in Spinoza, or Böehme, or Comte. Using the term in its metaphysical sense, we aim not to be partialists but universalists of inquiry and knowledge. We consider all Scriptures as literature; we hold that experience is the measure and method of revelation; and that, for the ripening of experience, man should be both individualized and insociated. Believers in the Divine Immanence, we hold by the "True Light, that lighteth every man who cometh into the world;" but we further conclude that the Creative Logos, "God manifested in the flesh," is not male merely, or female merely, but the two-in-one. The doctrine of the Divine-human Two-in-One, in whose individual and social likeness, in whose spiritual and physical likeness, we seek to be re-born, is the pivot of our faith and the directive force of our life. The ages wait for the manifestation of the sons of God. Thus we are adventists, not in a sectarian sense, but in the sense of a divine involution, and thence of a new degree in human evolution. Our faith teaches us love for all men, however inverted, arrested, or infirm, as our dear brethren. Our sympathies are especially toward those who have devoted themselves, in a practical sense, to the substitution of "altruism" for egoism, of mutuality for competition, in social life.

With these views you will readily perceive why the Brotherhood of the New Life has both sought to maintain a modest privacy, and to keep aloof from the prevalent discussions of social amelioration and reform.

With kind regards, believe me

Faithfully yours,   T. L. HARRIS.

In Dr. Taylor's "History of the Town of Portland," referred to in the preceding communication, we find a chapter devoted to the "Brotherhood of the New Life," which includes a letter from Mr. Harris, from which we take the following paragraphs:

"The purchase made by myself and friends in the town of Portland consists of something less than two thousand acres, principally of farm and vineyard lands, but inclusive of the plat at the junction of the Lake Shore and Alleghany Valley railroad, where we are laying out a village which we have named Salem-on-Erie, designing to make it an industrial and business center. These properties were secured mainly in the month of October, 1867; about one-half as a personal investment, and the moiety in behalf of the gentlemen interested with me in the enterprise. These lands in part comprise what is known on the old town maps as 'the Diamond,' and extend in length two miles on the shore of Lake Erie, being nearly contiguous to each other.

"Besides the usual operations in agriculture and vine-culture, we are engaged, first, in the wholesale pressing and shipping of hay; second, in the general nursery business; third, in the manufacture and sale of pure native wines, more especially for medicinal use. Our product of wines is from fifteen thousand to twenty-three thousand gallons annually. Our principal cellar is of stone, arched and fire-proof, 110 feet in length, and affording, with the one adjoining, storage for about 65,000 gallons of wine. At the village we also carry on a hotel and restaurant, and have just enlarged our operations by erecting a steam grist-mill and opening an exchange for transactions in produce and general merchandise. We are at present laying out and planting a public park and gardens, and draining and improving, as well as from time to time adding to, the freehold estate."

These statistics need considerable modification to express the present truth, the Brotherhood having, as Mr. Harris says in his letter on a previous page, contracted its business at Salem-on-Erie within the past few years. Indeed, I found on the occasion of my visit, a little more than a year ago, the hotel and store of the Brotherhood closed, their railway restaurant burnt, and neither their vine-culture nor other businesses in a very flourishing condition. Some of the estate had been sold, and the impression prevailed that they would gladly dispose of more. Part of the Family had followed their leader to California, and others, it was thought, were intending to take up their line of march for the same destination. All this, however, furnishes no evidence that the Brotherhood is losing ground in numbers or property: it may be only "changing its base of operations."

Mr. Harris says further in his letter to Dr. Taylor:

"The one object of the Brotherhood is the realization of the noble Christian ideal in social service. It is simply an effort to demonstrate that the ethical creed of the Gospel is susceptible of service as a working system, adapted to the complex and cultured nineteenth century, and containing the practical solution of the social problems of the age. In one sense the Brotherhood are Spiritualists: in the fervid and intense conviction that the individual man has no real life in himself; that all life, and with it the virtues and energies of life, are the result of a divine inflowing. Considering, first, that all real life is the continuous outgift of God, and, second, that our Lord is that one pure and living God (whether right or wrong in their opinion), there is among them a practical faith in him as the sole Ruler, Actuator and Director. They are monarchists, who recognize the Divine Man for their Sovereign.

"In another sense the Brotherhood are Socialists. They consider that the practical fulfillment of the Gospel is in what may be termed 'Divine-natural Society.' From the present civilization, the aggregation of self-interests, they would evolve a noble form, 'one pure and perfect chrysolite'—the association of noble and cultured souls in every industrial and human service. They hold most fully and most vitally, that the 'worship of God is the service of humanity.' If they revere in Christ the Lord, they also accept in him the Artisan.

"While they do not reject the sacred observance of accustomed Religion, they believe in uplifting every avocation of life into a permanent Religious Ministration. Cherishing the faith of Scripture in individual regeneration, they hold that it is the function of regenerate man to regenerate society; that this work must be initiated and carried out by the entrance of the cultured, the prosperous, the gifted, as well as those of humbler state, into those employments which have been counted menial; and that those labors should be done from the inspiration of the Divine Love which have heretofore been performed from selfish greed or at the mere spur of material necessity. 'See,' said the ancient pagans, 'how these Christians love one another.' It is the aim of the Brotherhood, in all its many fields of action, to re-instate that antique and eternal principle, not in demonstrative preachment, but in a most unobtrusive yet demonstrated social fact."

Dr. Taylor does not add many particulars of interest. He

mentions that sixty-five or seventy are engaged upon the Portland purchase, and adds: "They live by themselves as far as possible, and are exceedingly reticent with reference to the association and its inner workings when approached by those outside, and will hold no converse with the simply curious. The fact of their being difficult of access excites curiosity, and is the occasion of much impertinent inquiry. The air and the charm of mystery hang over and about them." And he concludes his chapter with the following testimonial in their favor:

"It is but just to say of the Brotherhood in Portland, that in all respects they seem to be living out the principles of their order in their every-day life, and regard their religion as something to be put on and worn as a garment. Their deportment is most discreet and gentlemanly, and although their interests seem to center, to a large extent, in their association, they are excellent citizens."

The Family at Fountain Grove in Santa Rosa, California, number at present about twenty persons. They have a beautiful location and rich, productive land; and their principal sources of income are the raising of hay, grain and other agricultural products.

For the benefit of those who would inform themselves more thoroughly respecting the principles of the Brotherhood, it may be added that they have recently published two pamphlets entitled, "The Lord, the Two-in-One," and "Hymns of the Two-in-One," and have also begun the publication of a journal called "*The Wedding Guest.*"

INDUCTIONS.

WE have given a description of the principal Communistic Societies of the United States. Let us inquire what is taught by the facts of their history.

They teach, in the first place, that it is possible to solve by methods free from strife the problem of the relations of labor and capital. In these Communities there exist no distinctions of rich and poor. All are laborers, and all are capitalists; and all seek the common interest. A "strike" on the one hand, and a "lockout" on the other, are made impossible by their fundamental principle of common property.

They teach that individual holding of property is not essential to industry and the vigorous prosecution of complicated businesses.

They teach that there are great advantages and economies in communal life.

They teach that a large proportion of what are termed middle-men, as also of non-producers in general, may be transferred to the side of production.

They teach that litigation and other expensive evils, made necessary, in part at least, by the system of individual property, disappear with the advent of Communism.

They teach that pauperism and trampism, necessary results of the grab-system, by which some are made extremely rich and others extremely poor, have no place in Communism.

They teach that education, libraries, lectures, the pleasures of art, the instructions of science, the best means of moral and spiritual discipline, may be brought within the reach of the common people.

They teach that the necessary preliminary conditions of successful Communism are comparatively few and within reach of all. None of the described Communities had at starting the numbers or capital required by Fourier, or any conception of the laws he deemed so indispensable. They have wrought out their success under the simple conviction that it is possible to live together and work together as brethren.

They teach that successful Communism is not dependent on any single theory of the sexual relation; for there are monogamic Communities as prosperous as the celibate ones, and others favoring complex-marriage as prosperous as those which hold to monogamy.

They teach that while no special religious system, or special interpretation of the Scriptures, is essential to success in Communism, RELIGION is a powerful promoter of AGREEMENT, which is indispensable to the permanent prosperity of any Community. The present anarchic condition of the Icarian Community emphasizes this fact, as does also the entire history of American Socialism.

They teach that in proportion as a Community loses the afflatus of its first leaders and relies upon doctrines and the machinery of government, it tends to death: in other words, a Community needs, for its growth and progress in all stages of its career, a living power at its center not inferior to that which it had in the beginning.

IN addition to the Communities already described, which have existed for a number of years, and attracted the attention of the public by their prosperity, there are quite a number of Socialistic experiments—Communistic, Fourieristic, Spiritualistic and Coöperative—in different parts of the country.

The "Adonai-Shomo" is the name of a Community which has existed for sixteen years in Athol, Mass. It has twelve members, owns 210 acres of land, and is reported to be financially prosperous. It has a religious foundation, bases its Communism of goods on the example and teachings of the Primitive Church, and observes the seventh day of the week as "the Sabbath of the Lord our God." It obtained a charter Jan. 1st, 1876. Asa F. Richards is President. Its Hebrew name signifies "the Lord, the Spirit, is there."

"The Home" is a Community of twelve persons located in Gilmore, Benzie County, Michigan, on a domain of 320 acres. It has a printed constitution and by-laws, and reports itself as slowly prospering. It has been founded but little more than a year.

There is a Community of about the same size in Kane County, Illinois, which has had a longer term of existence.

There is another Community of a dozen persons, mostly of the same family, at Plattsburgh, Missouri.

Alcander Longley is starting a Community in Bollinger County of the same State.

The Progressive Community at Cedar Vale, Chautauqua

County, Kansas, has a total membership of ten persons.

In Urbana, Neosho County, Kansas, there is an organization called the Esperanza Community, which publishes monthly "*The Star of Hope.*"

A Community is just starting at Ancora, New Jersey, under the leadership of Thomas Austin; and a small Society with some Communistic features has for a short period been in practical operation in the same place under Samuel Fowler.

Tappan Townsend, Samuel Leavitt, J. H. Ingalls and others are proposing to establish "A Hotel and Cottage Association" on a tract of twenty acres at Falls Glen, near Fanwood, New Jersey, twenty miles from New York City.

The "Springfield Industrial Works," of Springfield, Vermont, now called the "Union Manufacturing Company," has attracted considerable attention. It is a Coöperative enterprise, including thirty or forty persons, with a Unitary Home and other Communistic features. Mr. J. A. H. Ellis is acting Superintendent.

The "Coöperative Industrial Association of Virginia" is a chartered company, that has secured lands on the bluffs of the Potomac, twenty miles from Washington. Thomas J. Durant is President and Dr. J. A. Rowland is Secretary—both of Washington, D. C. This enterprise has not made great practical progress, and does not contemplate any form of Communism. It states its objects to be "to organize labor and social life upon the basis of order and justice—to secure higher education, fuller protection and better conditions of living."

There are two or more schemes for establishing Communal or Coöperative homes in Florida, and a few Socialists have recently secured four hundred acres in that State for this purpose, but have not yet published their plans. A company has been organized in New York and Brooklyn, calling itself the

"St. John's Coöperative Colony of Florida," which proposes to purchase ten thousand acres of land in that State.

A company is organizing in Massachusetts for the systematic planting of Coöperative Colonies in the Western States.

Another company is forming in St. Louis for the purpose of establishing Coöperative Colonies in Texas. Their plan, as at present explained, contemplates that "the whole community will labor in the Coöperative way, and will be governed by laws made by themselves.

Colorado has the flourishing city of Greeley, which was founded on the Coöperative plan and has many Coöperative features. Though it has had a growth of only eight years it now has eighteen hundred inhabitants, with fine churches, school-houses and other public buildings, and is surrounded with a still larger agricultural population. "Coöperation," says a recent visitor at Greeley, "has made production, and consequently living, from 25 to 40 per cent. cheaper here than elsewhere in Colorado. The Coöperative principles have been applied in the general, leaving the details to be worked out by individual efforts. In the wholesale purchase of land, fencing and irrigation, several hundred thousand dollars were saved, and now the annual interest on that amount. The people own the lands, the water, the fences, the village and all the privileges Coöperation has secured them. These conditions and privileges which accompany the farms are as much a part of them as the foundation rocks. A board of trustees is elected annually, a superintendent of canals and fences employed, and assessments levied every year to meet all expenses. The people are justly proud of their record. They have no poor, no criminals, no idle loafers, and no police. To-day this village and Community are the most prosperous in Colorado. Here 4,000 people have found happy homes, and form the nucleus of what shall be in time 50,000 population."

California has several Coöperative settlements, of which Anaheim is best known and most flourishing. The 1,165 acres purchased there twenty years ago at $2 per acre, by fifty poor German mechanics, have been increased to 3,200 acres, and their value enhanced more than fifteen-fold on the average, and in some cases more than an hundred-fold. It was, however, Coöperative only during the first years of its history.

"Prairie Home," or "Silkville," in Franklin County, Kansas, founded by E. V. Boissière, a French gentleman of wealth and culture, is one of the most interesting experiments now in progress. M. Boissière has here invested in land, buildings, etc., over one hundred thousand dollars, which he proposes to devote to "Association and Coöperation based on Attractive Industry." His scheme, so far as it is developed, appears to be a modified form of Fourierism. He proposes "as a leading feature of the enterprise to establish the 'Combined Household' of Fourier—that is, a single large residence for all the associates." And he states that his principal aim is "to organize labor, the source of all wealth, first, on the basis of remuneration proportioned to production; and second, in such manner as to make it both efficient and attractive. Guarantees of education and subsistence to all, and of help to those who need it, are indispensable conditions, to be provided as soon as the organization shall be sufficiently advanced to render them practicable." Several buildings have been erected, and some industries started, as farming, fruit-growing and silk-culture. But *festina lente* is the motto of both M. Boissière and of his able assistant, Mr. Charles Sears. They wisely choose to thoroughly mature their plans and test them on the small scale before largely advertising their experiment.

There are numerous Coöperative stores and Coöperative

manufacturing companies in the Northern States, and even large Orders, like the Grangers and Sovereigns of Industry, and a Socialist Labor Party, that might be mentioned in this connection as additional evidences that a tidal wave of Socialism—using this term in its broadest sense—is bearing society onward toward conditions more accordant with its ultimate destiny.

CHARACTERISTICS OF AMERICAN COMMUNISM.

IMMENSE mischief is done by the confounding of things in popular estimation which are distinct in character and object. This most often occurs when two things happen to have some peculiarities in common, and hence a common name. For example, the American people, a century ago, established a republican form of government, which was peaceable, orderly, and remarkably free from excesses of all kinds. Scarcely had their work been completed when the French people also undertook the same task. Their effort was premature, and the result shocking to men and angels. Their republic was soon transformed into a military despotism, but during its short term of existence, under the name of liberty and of republicanism, the greatest disorder and most horrible excesses prevailed. It should have been plain to all the world that the republicanism of Marat and Danton, St. Just and

Robespierre, was a wholly different thing from the republicanism of Adams and Franklin, Jefferson and Washington; but the monarchists of Europe and the tories of the United States and the opponents of republicanism every-where persistently confounded the two, and compelled the lovers of liberty here to suffer the opprobrium which belonged solely to the political demagogues and fanatics of France. "Behold," they continually cried, "the fruits which grow on your boasted tree of liberty." And it was a long time before a clear distinction was recognized and expressed in the world's thought and language; but finally the republicanism of 1776 came to be known as *American*, in contradistinction from that of 1789, which was labelled *French*.

Communism is another unfortunate word, whose history has been similar to that of republicanism. America took the lead in the establishment of certain organizations, like the Shakers and Harmonists, based on Communism of property, and hence called Communities. Other Communities followed, successful and otherwise, but all carrying on their experiments without interference with common society or hostility to it. This was the normal character of American Communism. It was free from every form of compulsion and conservative of property, order and morality. It aimed to improve the present social condition of the world, but it relied mainly upon example, and asked only voluntary individual coöperation, and contemplated no violent or sudden revolutions in society. These facts were becoming recognized, and the word Communism was in a fair way to acquire honor if not renown, when, lo! another form of Communism entered the field, as widely contrasting with its American namesake as the American republicanism of 1776 contrasted with the French republicanism of 1789. This new form of Communism demanded that society as a whole should at once resolve itself into a state of common property, which would really be compulsory Communism, and would amount to plunder of the upper classes by the lower. Moreover, it would necessarily result in anarchy and enormous waste, if it did not end in universal poverty. It aimed at controlling all the functions of government and society. In a word, it was the Communism of force. It manifested itself on a large scale and displayed these inherent characteristics in France during and immediately following the Franco-Prussian war, and hence has been called French Communism. It showed itself in other countries, and was called European Communism, International Communism, etc. It may not deserve condemnation as wholly wrong in character, tendency and objects; but so far as it seeks its ends by compulsory means it is not allied to what is properly termed American Communism. There is reason to hope it will outgrow its objectionable features, as French republicanism has outgrown its original characteristics, but until it does there is no fairness in confounding the two kinds of Communism. The Communism which has been practically illustrated in the United States during the last four score years is voluntary, peaceable, conservative. From it there is no violence to be feared. If there is a "strike" or "outbreak" or "uprising" or "mob" or "disorder" or "destruction" anywhere or of any kind, it may be safely assumed that Communism, in the true American sense of the word, is in no manner responsible for it. It abhors all forms of compulsion.

THE COMMUNISTIC STANDARD OF CHARACTER.

MEN'S characters are determined in a great degree by their dominant aims, and these in the past ages of the world have been, for the most part, of a nature to unfit them for close organization. Personal distinction in one form or another has been and is the leading object of ambition among all classes and peoples. It matters little whether it is sought in war or trade, literature or art; its effect on personal character is essentially the same in all cases. Character thus developed cannot stand the test of Communism. It is in its very nature selfish and inorganic. The character demanded by Communism contrasts very sharply with that which gains the prizes in this world. It is outlined in the beatitudes of Christ and in Paul's description of charity. Those possessing it will strive neither for leadership nor for individual gain, but for peace, for the happiness of others, for personal improvement—for meekness, love, purity, righteousness.

The small family may have wealth, and all that wealth can procure; genius, and all that genius can achieve; and yet lack the essential elements of a happy home. There must be that which promotes love and unity; that which delights in serving others; that which avoids giving offense and does not easily take offense; that which yields readily to the judgment and wishes of others: these are the indispensable conditions of a happy home whether in hut or palace. And it is utter folly to suppose that a large family or Community can get along harmoniously without the same conditions. It may have its hundreds of members; its phalanstery; its groups and series; its immense domain; its manifold industries; its large library and every aid to intellectual development; and yet, unless it finds a way to secure the conditions enumerated as essential to the happiness of a small family, it will prove a gigantic failure. Indeed these conditions are more indispensable in a Community than anywhere else. The members of the common family have a large part of their association with persons outside of their circle; business, education, politics, religion, are continually bringing them into other combinations. But a Community, as a writer in the *Boston Commonwealth* has happily said, "is a church which clothes and feeds its members in a material as well as a spiritual sense:" it is more; it is a school which educates its members, a village in its industries and amusements; and it is a home that contemplates no dissolution. Its members have taken each other "for better, for worse," for life. They look not forward to the time when their organization will be broken by any of the agencies that disintegrate the common family. How unspeakably important it is, then, that in this perpetual home those characteristics should predominate which tend to harmony and brotherhood!

COMMUNITY LEADERSHIP.

IT is remarkable how many persons there are who conceive themselves well qualified to manage Communities. Men who have failed as lawyers and doctors and ministers, and even as ordinary business men, will not hesitate a moment to undertake the superintendence of a large Community. Poor leadership was doubtless a more potent cause of failure in the disastrous campaign of Fourierism than any or all of the causes commonly assigned, such as poor land, lack of capital, inadequate numbers. One of the most eloquent advocates of Fourierism and a director in two of its Phalanxes says, "None but high and commanding leaders could have reduced the crowds who sought entrance into these experiments to order, and such leaders they did not have;" and Horace Greeley, who in so many ways aided the Associations that were started, contributes this sketch of the class of persons who sought to control them: "They may have failed again and again and been protested at every bank to which they have been presented; yet they are sure to jump into any new movement as if they had been born expressly to superintend and direct it, though they are morally certain to ruin whatever they lay their hands on. Destitute of means, of practical ability, of prudence, tact and common sense, they have such a wealth of assurance and self confidence that they clutch the responsible positions which the capable and worthy modestly shrink from; so responsibilities that would task the ablest are mistakenly devolved on the blindest and least fit. Many an experiment is thus wrecked, when, engineered by its best members, it might have succeeded."

It is utterly futile to undertake the establishment of Communities unless men can be found to lead them who have at least as much ability and intelligence as is required, for instance, in the successful management of a railroad or bank or large manufactory. They must also possess other and more rare qualifications, such as freedom from selfish ambition and the genuine spirit of service. Christ said to his disciples: "Ye know that the princes of the Gentiles exercise dominion over them, and they that are great exercise authority upon them. But it shall not be so among you; but whosoever will be greatest among you let him be your minister; and whosoever will be chief among you let him be your servant." That is the kind of leadership for Communities—a kind that makes harmony rather than strife. The more leaders of this sort there are the better. If a man honestly labors as a servant of the Community, and grows great in its service, the well-disposed will rejoice in his prosperity as they would in their own.

The best leaders will be given to meditation, searching into interior truth, and in their intercourse with the Community will be, not chiefly commanders and directors, but instructors and teachers of interior things. Leadership which consists mainly in the exercise of personal influence, however great the person who exercises it, tends to bondage; and the greater the person the greater the bondage. "If I bring out a principle," says one who has thought much on these deep questions, "your loyalty is spontaneous to that, and the truth does not bring you into bondage. If I show you how to do an example in arithmetic, you do not have to look to me, or be governed by me, in doing it; the truth is sufficient of itself to attract and govern you." Leadership that relies mainly upon the truth for its means of influence and government will never become oppressive.

With the right standard of character for both leaders and led, it will be an easy task to multiply Communities in all civilized lands.

APPENDIX.

ARTICLES OF ASSOCIATION OF THE HARMONY SOCIETY.

WHEREAS, by the favor of Divine Providence, an Association or Community has been formed by George Rapp and many others, upon the basis of Christian fellowship, the principles of which, being faithfully derived from the sacred Scriptures, include the government of the patriarchal age, united to the Community of property, adopted in the days of the apostles, and wherein the simple object sought is to approximate, so far as human imperfections may allow, to the fulfillment of the will of God, by the exercise of those affections and the practice of those virtues which are essential to the happiness of man in time and throughout eternity;

And whereas, it is necessary to the good order and well-being of the said Association, that the conditions of membership should be clearly understood, and that the rights, privileges and duties of every individual therein should be so defined as to prevent mistake or disappointment on the one hand, and contention or disagreement on the other;

Therefore be it known to all whom it may concern, that we, the undersigned, citizens of the County of Beaver, in the Commonwealth of Pennsylvania, do severally and distinctly, each for himself, covenant, grant and agree, to and with the said George Rapp and his associates as follows, viz.:

ARTICLE 1st. We, the undersigned, for ourselves, our heirs, executors and administrators, do hereby give, grant, and forever convey to the said George Rapp and his associates, and to their heirs and assigns, all our property, real, personal and mixed, whether it be lands and tenements, goods and chattels, money or debts due to us, jointly or severally in possession, in remainder, or in reversion or expectancy, whatsoever and wheresoever, without evasion, qualification or reserve, as a free gift or donation, for the benefit and use of the said Association or Community, and we do hereby bind ourselves, our heirs, executors and administrators, to do all such other acts as may be necessary to vest a perfect title to the same in the said Association, and to place the said property at the full disposal of the superintendent of the said Community without delay.

ARTICLE 2d. We do further covenant and agree to and with the said George Rapp and his associates, that we will severally submit faithfully to the laws and regulations of said Community, and will at all times manifest a ready and cheerful obedience toward those who are or may be appointed as superintendents thereof, holding ourselves bound to promote the interest and welfare of the said Community, not only by the labor of our own hands, but also by that of our children, our families, and all others who now are, or hereafter may be, under our control.

ARTICLE 3d. If, contrary to our expectations, it should so happen that we could not render the faithful obedience aforesaid, and should be induced from that or any other cause to withdraw from the said Association, then and in such case we do expressly covenant and agree to and with the said George Rapp and his associates, that we never will claim or demand, either for ourselves or our children, or for any one belonging to us, directly or indirectly, any compensation, wages or reward whatever for our or their labor or services rendered to the said Community, or to any member thereof, but whatever we or our families jointly or severally shall or may do, all shall be held and considered as a voluntary service for our brethren.

ARTICLE 4th. In consideration of the premises, the said George Rapp and his associates do, by these presents, adopt the undersigned jointly and severally, as members of the said Community, whereby each of them obtains the privilege of being present at every religious meeting and receiving, not only for themselves but also for their children and families, all such instructions in church and school as may be reasonably required both for their temporal good and for their eternal felicity.

ARTICLE 5th. The said George Rapp and his associates further agree to supply the undersigned severally with all the necessaries of life, as clothing, meat, drink, lodging, etc., for themselves and their families. And this provision is not limited to their days of health and strength; but when any of them shall become sick, infirm, or otherwise unfit for labor, the same support and maintenance shall be allowed as before, together with such medicine, care, attendance, and consolation, as their situation may reasonably demand. And if at any time after they have become members of the Association, the father or mother of a family should die or be otherwise separated from the Community and should leave their family behind, such family shall not be left orphans or destitute, but shall partake of the same rights and maintenance as before, so long as they remain in the Association, as well in sickness as in health, and to such extent as their circumstances may require.

ARTICLE 6th. And if it should so happen as above mentioned, that any of the undersigned should violate his or their agreement, and would or could not submit to the laws and regulations of the Church or the Community, and for that or any other cause should withdraw from the Association, then the said George Rapp and his associates agree to refund to him or them the value of all such property as he or they may have brought into the Community, in compliance with the first article of this agreement, the said value to be refunded without interest, in one, two or three annual installments, as the said George Rapp and his associates shall determine. And if the person or persons so withdrawing themselves were poor, and brought nothing into the Community, notwithstanding, if they depart openly and regularly, they shall receive a donation in money, according to the length of their stay, and to their conduct, and to such amount as their necessities may require, in the judgment of the superintendents of the Association.

The provision in regard to refunding property to seceders was abrogated in 1836 by the unanimous adoption of the following additional articles :

1st. The said sixth article [in regard to refunding] is entirely annulled and made void, as if it had never existed, all others to remain in full force as heretofore. 2d. All the property of the Society, real, personal and mixed, in law or equity, and howsoever contributed or acquired, shall be deemed now and forever joint and indivisible stock. Each individual is to be considered to have finally and irrevocably parted with all his former contributions, whether in lands, goods, money or labor, and the same rule shall apply to all future contributions, whatever they may be. 3d. Should any individual withdraw from the Society, or depart this life, neither he in the one case, nor his representatives in the other, shall be entitled to demand an account of said contributions, or to claim any thing from the Society as a matter of right ; but it shall be left altogether to the discretion of the superintendent to decide whether any, and if any, what allowance shall be made to such member, or his representatives, as a donation.

ARTICLES OF ASSOCIATION OF THE COMMUNITY AT ZOAR, OHIO.

ARTICLES OF THE FIRST CLASS.

We, the undersigned, members of the First Class of Separatists, party of the first part, and George Gasely, Jacob Ackermann and Christian Ruof, Trustees elect, and their successors in office, of the Separatists' Society of Zoar, in the County of Tuscarawas, and State of Ohio, party of the second part, have, through confidence mutually reposed in one another, established, and by these presents do establish, the following rules and principles of social compact, for the better fulfillment of the duties of mankind, which we owe one another, and also for the furtherance of our spiritual and temporal welfare and happiness.

ARTICLE 1st. We, the said party of the first part, do declare, that by our own free will and accord we have agreed, and by these presents do agree, and bind ourselves to labor, obey, and execute all the orders of said Trustees and their successors in office ; and from the day of the date hereof henceforth to use all our industry and skill in behalf of the exclusive benefit and welfare of the said Separatists' Society of Zoar, and continue to do so as long as strength and health will permit, to the entire satisfaction of said Trustees and their successors in office.

ARTICLE 2d. And we do also hereby agree and bind ourselves firmly by these presents, to put our minor children under the care and control of the said Trustees and their successors in office, in the same manner as if they had been bound by indentures to serve and dwell with them and their successors in office, for and during the term of their minority, subject to all the duties, and likewise entitled to the same rights and protection, as indentured children by law are subject and entitled to, until they shall have attained their proper age, as defined by the statutes of the State of Ohio.

ARTICLE 3d. And the said Trustees do hereby, for themselves and their successors in office, agree and bind themselves to furnish the said party of the first part with suitable dwelling, board and clothing, free of cost, the clothing to consist at any time of no less than two suits, including the clothes brought by the said party of the first part to this Society; and in case of sickness, necessary care and attendance is hereby promised to the said party of the first part; and this performance of the Trustees and their successors in office shall be considered by the party of the first part a full compensation for all their labors and services, done, either by themselves or their minor children, without any further claim or demands whatever.

ARTICLE 4th. Good and moral behavior, such as is enjoined by strict observance of the principles of Holy Writ, are by both parties hereby promised to be observed; hence it is clearly understood that all profane language, immoral words and acts, which may cause offense amongst the other members of this Community, are not only wholly to be avoided, but, on the contrary, all are to endeavor to set good examples and to cherish general and mutual love.

ARTICLE 5th. The object of this agreement being, furthermore, to preserve peace and unity, and as such can only be maintained by a general equality among its members, it is therefore severally understood and declared, that no extra demands shall be made or allowed in respect to meat, drink, clothing, dwellings, etc. (cases of sickness excepted), but such, if any can be allowed to exist, may and shall be obtained by individuals through means of their own, and never out of the common fund.

ARTICLE 6th. All monies which the said party of the first part either now possess, or hereafter may receive into their possession, shall without delay be deposited in the common fund of this Society, for which a receipt, payable on demand, is to be given; but upon the request of said party of the first part, in order to procure extra necessaries, as the case may be, a part or the whole of said deposit shall be refunded to the owner.

ARTICLE 7th. All manner of misunderstandings and differences shall be settled by way of arbitration, and not otherwise, that is, by a body of three or five persons, to be chosen by both parties; and their decision shall be held binding upon both parties.

Article 8th. All rules and regulations contained in the foregoing articles (if any there be that are not plain enough, or are subject to misapprehension), shall be so understood as never to be in opposition to, but always in perfect accordance with, the morals, usages, principles and regulations of the members of the Second Class of the Separatists' Society of Zoar.

Article 9th. These articles being fully and fairly understood, to their strict and faithful performance both parties bind themselves in the most solemn manner, jointly and severally, their children, heirs, executors, administrators and successors in office, by the penal sum of fifty dollars, current money of the United States of North America.

Article 10th. If in consequence of the foregoing, a penalty upon any one of the parties to this agreement shall be laid, then, in case of refusal or non-compliance, the party so refusing may be prosecuted for the same before any magistrate or Justice of the Peace in the Township, County and State wherein the defendant may reside, and judgment shall be had agreeable to the laws of this State; and said magistrate or Justice of the Peace shall forthwith proceed to collect such penalty, and pay it over to the party who by law is entitled to the same. In testimony whereof, both parties have hereunto set their hands and seals this 14th day of October in the year of our Lord, 1833.

———

FULL COVENANT OF THE MEMBERS OF THE SECOND CLASS.

We, the subscribers, members of the Society of Separatists of the Second Class, declare hereby that we give all our property, of every kind, not only what we possess, but what we may hereafter come in possession of by inheritance, gift, or otherwise, real or personal, and all rights, titles, and expectations whatever, both for ourselves and our heirs, to the said Society forever, to be and remain, not only during our lives, but after our deaths, the exclusive property of the Society. Also we promise and bind ourselves to obey all the commands and orders of the Trustees and their subordinates, with the utmost zeal and diligence, without opposition or grumbling; and to devote all our strength, good-will, diligence and skill, during our whole lives, to the common service of the Society and for the satisfaction of its Trustees. Also we consign in a similar manner our children, so long as they are minors, to the charge of the Trustees, giving these the same rights and powers over them as though they had been formally indentured to them under the laws of the State.

COVENANT OF THE ONEIDA COMMUNITY.

WHEREAS, the Society called the Oneida Community, having its head-quarters at or near the village of Oneida, County of Madison, and State of New York, and branches at Wallingford, State of Connecticut, and other places, was founded by John H. Noyes and others for the purpose of religious fellowship and discipline; and

WHEREAS, it has been and is the agreement of the members of the said Oneida Community, and of all its branches, by and with one another, that on the admission of any member all property belonging to him or her becomes the joint-property of the Community, and of all its members, and the education, subsistence, clothing, and other necessaries of life furnished to members and their children in the Community are agreed and held to be just equivalents for all labor performed, and services rendered, and property contributed, no accounts being kept between any member and the Community, or between individual members, and no claim for wages accruing to him or her in case of subsequent withdrawal; and

WHEREAS, it has heretofore been the practice of the Community to keep a record of the estimated amount or value of the property put in by every member joining the Community, and to refund the same or an equivalent amount or value, without interest, use, or increase, in case of the subsequent voluntary withdrawal of the member;

YET, as this practice stands and has already stood on the ground, not of obligation, but of good will and liberality, the time and manner of refunding such property or its value resting entirely in the discretion of the Community through the voice of its members, who may also discontinue this custom of refunding at any time they see fit, or refuse in any case to refund all or any part of such property contributed by any member, upon or after his or her withdrawal, at their pleasure; and

WHEREAS, it is also agreed that on the death of a member, or his or her expulsion for just cause, the Community, its trustees, officers, or other representatives, are not bound to refund all or any part of the property contributed by such members to his heirs, executors, administrators, or assigns;

THEREFORE, we, the undersigned, acknowledge the above as the terms of our connection with and membership in the Oneida Community and all its branches now existing or that may hereafter exist, and we severally, for ourselves, our heirs, executors, administrators, and assigns, do agree and covenant with it, and with its members, and with one another, and with the present property-holders thereof, and their successors in office, that neither we nor our heirs, executors, administrators, nor assigns, will ever bring any action, either at law or in equity, or other process or proceeding whatsoever, against said Community or its branches, or against the agents, or property-holders thereof, or any person or corporation, for wages or other compensation for service, nor for the recovery of any property by us or either of us contributed to the funds or property of said Community or its branches, on or before our entering the same, or at any subsequent time, nor make any claim or demand therefor, of any kind or nature whatsoever.

THE SHAKER COVENANT.

[We omit the preamble of this Covenant, and such parts as relate to the objects of the Society and the duties of the subordinate officers.]

ORDER AND OFFICE OF THE MINISTRY.

We acknowledge and declare that for the purpose of promoting and maintaining union, order and harmony throughout the various branches of this Community, the primary administration of parental authority has been settled in the first established Ministry at Mt. Lebanon, N. Y., there to rest and remain as the center of union to all who are in Gospel relation and communion with the Society. The established order of this Ministry includes four persons ; two of each sex.

PERPETUITY OF THEIR OFFICE AND HOW SUPPLIED.

We further acknowledge and declare that the said primary administration of parental authority has been and is perpetuated as follows: Namely, that the first in that office and calling possesses the right given by the sanction of divine authority, through the first founders of this Society, to prescribe or direct any regulation or appointment which they may judge most proper and necessary respecting the Ministry or any other important matter which may concern the welfare of the Church subsequent to their decease. But in case no such regulation or appointment be so prescribed or directed, then the right to direct and authorize such regulation and appointment devolves upon the surviving members of the Ministry, in council with the Elders of the Church, or others, as the nature of the case in their judgment may require. Such appointments being officially communicated to all concerned, and receiving the general approbation of the Church, are confirmed and supported in the Society.

THE MINISTERIAL OFFICE IN THE SEVERAL SOCIETIES.

We further acknowledge and declare, covenant and agree that the ministerial office and authority in any Society or Community of our faith, which has emanated or which may emanate, in a regular line of *order from* the center of union aforesaid, is, and shall be acknowledged, owned and respected as, the spiritual and primary authority of such Society or Community in all matters pertaining to the ministerial office. And in case of the decease or removal of any individual of said Ministry, in any such Society, his or her lot and place shall be filled by agreement of the surviving Ministers, in council with the Elders and others, as the nature of the case may require, together with the knowledge and approbation of the primary ministerial authority at Mt. Lebanon, N. Y., aforesaid, to which they are responsible.

POWERS AND DUTIES OF THE MINISTRY.

The Ministry being appointed and established as aforesaid are vested with the primary authority of the Church and its various branches. Hence, it becomes their special duty to guide and superintend the spiritual concerns of the Society as a body of people under their care and government, and in connection with the Elders in their respective families and departments, who shall act in union with them, to give and establish such orders, rules and regulations as may be found necessary for the government and protection of the Church and Society within the limits of their jurisdiction, and also to counsel, advise and judge in all matters of importance, whether spiritual or temporal. The said Ministry are also vested with authority, in connection with the Elders as aforesaid, to nominate and appoint to office Ministers, Elders, Deacons, and Trustees, and to assign offices of care and trust to such brethren and sisters as they, the said Ministry and Elders, shall judge to be best qualified for the several offices to which they may be appointed; and we do hereby covenant and agree that such nominations and appointments, being made and officially communicated to those concerned, and receiving the general approbation of the Church, or of the Families concerned, shall thenceforth be confirmed and supported until altered or revoked by the authority aforesaid.

PREPARATION FOR ADMISSION INTO CHURCH RELATION.

In order that believers may be prepared for entering into the sacred privilege of Church relation, it is of primary importance that sufficient opportunity and privilege should be afforded under the ministry of the Gospel for them to acquire suitable instruction in the genuine principles of righteousness, honesty, justice and true holiness, and also that they should prove their faith and Christian morality by their practical obedience to the precepts of the Gospel according to their instructions. It is also indispensably necessary for them to receive the one uniting spirit of Christ, and to become so far of one heart and one mind that they are willing to sacrifice all other relations for this sacred *one.* Another essential step is to settle all just and equitable claims of creditors and *filial* heirs, so that whatever property they may possess shall be justly their own. When this is done, and they feel themselves sufficiently prepared to make a deliberate and final choice, to devote themselves, with all they possess. wholly to the service of God, without reserve, and it shall be deemed proper by the leading authority of the Church, after examination and due consideration, to allow them to associate together in the capacity of a Church, or a branch thereof in Gospel order, they may then consecrate themselves and all they possess to the service of God forever, and confirm the same by signing and sealing a written covenant predicated upon the principles herein contained, and fulfilling, on their part, all its obligations.

ADMISSION OF NEW MEMBERS.

As the door must be kept open for the admission of new members into the Church, when duly prepared, it is agreed that each and every person who shall at any time after the date and execution of the Church Covenant, in any branch of the Community, be admitted into the Church as a member thereof, shall previously have a fair opportunity to obtain a full, clear and explicit understanding of the object and design of the Church Covenant, and of the obligations it enjoins upon the members. For this purpose, he or she shall, in the presence of two of the Deacons or acting Trustees of the Church, read, or hear the same distinctly read, so as to be able freely to acknowledge his or her full approbation and acceptance thereof, in all its parts. Then he, she or they (as the case may be), shall be at liberty to sign the same ; and having signed and sealed it, and being subject to all the obligations required of the original signers, shall thenceforth be entitled to all the benefits and privileges thereunto appertaining ; and the signature or signatures thus added shall be certified by the said Deacons or Trustees, together with the date thereof.

PRIVILEGES AND OBLIGATIONS OF MEMBERS.

The united interests of the Church having been formed and established by the free-will offerings and pious donations of the members respectively, from the commencement of the institution, for the object and purposes already stated, it cannot be considered either as a joint-tenancy or a tenancy in common, but as a *consecrated whole*, designed for and devoted to the uses and purposes of the Gospel forever, agreeable to the established principles of the Church: Therefore it shall be held, possessed and enjoyed by the Church, in their united capacity, as a sacred and covenant right: That is to say, all and every member thereof, while standing in Gospel union and maintaining the principles of this Covenant, *shall enjoy equal rights, benefits and privileges, in the use of all things pertaining to the Church, according to their several needs and circumstances;* and no difference shall be made on account of what any one has contributed and devoted, or may hereafter contribute and devote to the support and benefit of the institution.

It is nevertheless stipulated and agreed that the benefits, privileges and enjoyments secured by this Covenant to the members of the Church, shall not be considered as extending to any person who shall refuse to comply with the conditions of this association ; or who shall refuse to submit to the admonition and discipline of the constituted authority of the Church ; or who shall willfully depart from the principles and practice of those religious and moral obligations which have been established in the Church, agreeable to the primitive faith and distinguished principles of this institution; of which refusal or non-compliance the leading authority acknowledged in the first article of this Covenant shall be the proper and constitutional judges.

OBLIGATIONS OF THE MEMBERS.

As subordination and obedience is the life and soul of every well-regulated Community, so our strength and protection, our happiness and prosperity, in our capacity of Church members, must depend on our faithful obedience to the rules and orders established in the Church, and to the instruction, counsel and advice of its leaders. Therefore, we do hereby covenant and agree that we will receive and acknowledge, as our Elders in the Gospel, those members in the Church who are or may be chosen and appointed for the time being to that office and calling by the authority aforesaid; and also that we will, as faithful brethren and sisters in Christ, conform and subject ourselves to the known and established faith and principles of our Community, and to the counsels and directions of the Elders, who shall act in union, as aforesaid, and also to all the orders, rules and regulations which are or may be given and established in the Church, according to the principles and by the authority aforesaid.

DUTIES OF THE MEMBERS.

The faithful improvement of our time and talents in doing good is a duty which God requires of man, as a rational, social and accountable being, and this duty is indispensable in the members of the Church of Christ. Therefore, it is and shall be required of all and every member of this institution, unitedly and individually, to occupy and improve their time and talents to support and maintain the interest of the Society, to promote the objects of this Covenant, and discharge their duty to God and each other according to their several abilities and callings, as members in union with one common lead; so that the various gifts and talents of all may be improved for the mutual benefit of each other and all concerned.

As we esteem the mutual possession and enjoyment of the consecrated interest and privileges of the Church a valuable consideration, fully adequate to any amount of personal interest, labor or service, devoted or consecrated by any individual; we, therefore, covenant and agree, in conformity with an established and well-known principle of the Church, that no person whatever under its care and protection can be employed for wages of any kind, on his or her individual account, and that no ground is or can be afforded for the recovery of any property or service devoted or consecrated as aforesaid; and it is also agreed that in case of the removal of any member or members from one Family, Society or branch of the Church to another, his, her or their previous signature or signatures to the Church or Family Covenant from whence such member or members shall have removed, shall forever bar all claims which are incompatible with the true intent and meaning of this Covenant, in the same manner as if such removal had not taken place. Yet all who shall so remove, in union with the authority aforesaid, shall be entitled to all the benefits and privileges of the Order in which they shall then be placed, so long as they shall conform to the rules and regulations of the same.

DEDICATION AND CONSECRATION OF PERSONS, PROPERTY AND SERVICE.

According to the faith of the Gospel which we have received, and agreeable to the uniform practice of the Church of Christ from its first establishment in this Society, we covenant and agree to dedicate, devote, consecrate and give up, and by this Covenant we do solemnly and conscientiously dedicate, devote, consecrate and give up ourselves and services, together with all our temporal interests to the service of God and the support and benefit of the Church of this Community, and to such other pious and charitable purposes as the Gospel may require, to be under the care and direction of such Elders, Deacons, and Trustees as are or may be appointed and established in the Church by the authority aforesaid.

DEDICATION AND RELEASE OF PRIVATE CLAIM.

Whereas, in pursuance of the requirement of the Gospel, and in the full exercise of our faith, reason and understanding, we have freely and voluntarily sacrificed all self-interest, and consecrated and devoted our persons, services and property, as aforesaid, to the pious and benevolent purposes of the Gospel: Therefore, we do hereby solemnly and conscientiously, unitedly and individually for ourselves and our heirs, release and quitclaim to the Deacons, or acting Trustees of the Church for the time being, for the uses and purposes aforesaid, all our private, personal right, title, interest, claim and demand of, in and to the estate, interest, property, and appurtenances so consecrated, devoted and given up; and we hereby jointly and severally promise and declare in the presence of God and before these witnesses, that we will never hereafter, neither directly nor indirectly, under any circumstances whatever, contrary to the stipulations of this Covenant, make nor require any account of any interest, property, labor nor service, nor any division thereof, which is, has been, or may be devoted by us, or any of us, to the uses and purposes aforesaid, nor bring any charge of debt or damage, nor hold any claim, nor demand whatever against the said Deacons or Trustees, nor against the Church or Society, nor against any member thereof, on account of any property or service given, rendered, devoted or consecrated to the aforesaid sacred and charitable purposes.

In confirmation of all the aforesaid statements, covenants, promises, and articles of agreement, we have hereunto subscribed our names and affixed our seals, commencing on this ——— day of ——— in the year of our Lord one thousand eight hundred and ———.